GLOBET

Travel

C000277517

STOCKHOLM
AND SWEDEN

RICHARD SALE

NEW
HOLLAND

NEW HOLLAND

> ★★★ Highly recommended
> ★★ Recommended
> ★ See if you can

First edition published in 2005
by New Holland Publishers (UK) Ltd
London • Cape Town • Sydney • Auckland
10 9 8 7 6 5 4 3 2 1

website: www.newhollandpublishers.com

Garfield House
86 Edgware Road
London W2 2EA
United Kingdom

80 McKenzie Street
Cape Town 8001
South Africa

14 Aquatic Drive
Frenchs Forest
NSW 2086
Australia

218 Lake Road
Northcote, Auckland
New Zealand

Distributed in the USA by
The Globe Pequot Press
Connecticut

ISBN 1 84330 652 2

Publishing Manager (UK): Simon Pooley
Publishing Manager (SA): Thea Grobbelaar
DTP Cartographic Manager: Genené Hart
Editor: Melany McCallum
Cartographer: Nicole Engeler
Design and DTP: Lellyn Creamer
Picture Researcher: Shavonne Johannes
Consultant: Hugh Taylor
Proofreader: Thea Grobbelaar
Reproduction by Hirt & Carter (Pty) Ltd, Cape Town
Printed and bound by Times Offset (M) Sdn. Bhd.,
Malaysia

Photographic Credits:
Alamy/Juliet Ferguson, page 114; **jonarold.com/
W.Bibikow**, page 96, **jonarold.com/G.Hellier**, page 113;
International Photobank/Peter Baker, cover, page 75;
Nicholas Sale, title page, pages 6, 9, 16, 18, 24, 26, 32, 40,
42, 45–47, 50, 53, 54, 56–58, 106, 108, 111; **Richard Sale**,
pages 4, 7, 13, 15, 17, 19-21, 25, 27, 30, 33, 36, 38, 43, 59, 60,
62, 65-69, 71, 72, 73, 78, 80, 90, 94, 95, 99, 101, 103, 116, 118;
Richard Sale Collection (SPRI), page 100; **SCPL/Dorothy
Burrows**, pages 12, 14, 88, 97; **SCPL/Stephen Coyne**, 29,
44; **SCPL/Joy Flood**, pages 77, 81, 109; **SCPL/Les Gibbon**,
pages 8, 10, 120; **SCPL/Kevin Harrison**, pages 22, 84, 86;
SCPL/Beresford Hills, page 92; **SCPL/Carola Holmberg**,
page 23; **SCPL/Elias Rostom**, page 55; **SCPL/Roy
Westlake**, page 34. [SCPL: Sylvia Cordaiy Photo Library;
SPRI: Swedish Polar Research Institute]

Acknowledgements:
The author would like to thank Nicholas Sale for his help
and for his hospitality in Stockholm.

Keep us Current:
Information in travel guides is apt to change, which is
why we regularly update our guides. We'd be grateful
to receive feedback if you've noted something we
should include in our updates. If you have new
information, please share it with us by writing to the
Publishing Manager, Globetrotter, at the office nearest
to you (addresses on this page). The most significant
contribution to each new edition will receive a free
copy of the updated guide.

Cover: *This replica Viking longboat tours the islands around
Stockholm. On evening cruises in summer, dinner is served.*
Title page: *In winter, an outdoor ice rink is created in
Kungsträdgården in central Stockholm.*

CONTENTS

1. Introducing Stockholm and Sweden 4
The Land 6
History in Brief 13
Government and Economy 20
The People 22

2. Stockholm 30
The History of Stockholm 31
Gamla Stan 33
Central Stockholm 36
Outer Stockholm 44
Around the Archipelago 45

3. Central Sweden 50
Uppland 52
Västmanland 55
Sörmland 57
Värmland 59

4. Southeast Sweden 62
Malmö 64
Lund 66
Landskrona 67
Helsingborg 68
The Far South 68
Kristianstad 71
Karlskrona 71
Kalmar 73
Öland 75
Glasriket 77
North Småland 78

Västervik 78
Vimmerby 79
Eksjö 79
Norrköping 79
Linköping 80
East of Lake Vättern 81

5. Gotland 84
Visby 86
The Island 87

6. Southwest Sweden 90
Gothenburg (Göteborg) 92
Bohuslän 95
Dalsland 97
Västergötland 98
Halland 102

7. Northern Sweden 106
Dalarna 108
Gästrikland 111
Sundsvall and Östersund 112
North to the Arctic 113

8. Lappland 116
Close to the Circle 118
Above the Circle 118

Travel Tips 122

Index 127

1
Introducing
Stockholm and Sweden

Mention Sweden and the images conjured up are of fair-skinned, blue-eyed blondes (and blonds), rampaging Vikings, Volvo and Saab, design and style. Often with such quick phrases reality is quite different from perception. This is not entirely the case in Sweden. All of the above are correct, though not all Swedes are blonde, the Vikings were mainly Danes and Norwegians, and Volvo and Saab are now owned by Ford and General Motors respectively. No one can argue with design and style. Sweden is one of the most stylish countries in Europe, a country where, it seems, all aspects of life have been examined to ensure that they improve the environment and the quality of life of ordinary people.

This respect for the environment is no surprise. Sweden is one of the most beautiful countries in the world, particularly the part that lies north of the Arctic Circle where some of Europe's finest national parks can be found, parks where bear and wolf still roam. It also has, in Stockholm, one of the most beautiful capital cities in the world. It is a fascinating place and has in the Vasa Museum one of the great museums of the world. In Visby, Sweden has one of the finest medieval cities in Europe, and that is just one of a host of historically interesting sites.

In straddling the Arctic Circle, Sweden can be thought of as existing in two worlds: to the south of the Arctic Circle is a European country, but to the north is a country where the midnight sun shines and the aurora borealis lights up the night sky. To complete

TOP ATTRACTIONS

*** Stockholm: a beautiful capital city; Gamla Stan and the Vasa Museum should be on everyone's list.
*** Sarek National Park: one of the best parks in Europe; fabulous scenery.
** Visby: superb medieval walled city.
* Göta Canal: a journey along it showcases some of the best of Sweden.
* Falun: the phenomenal remains of one of the world's most important copper mines.

Opposite: *The canal around Malmö's castle, the Malmöhus, frozen in midwinter.*

FACTS AND FIGURES

Area: 450,000km² (175,000 sq. miles); about the same size as Germany and Austria combined. Top to bottom, Sweden is very long – 1575km (980 miles) from north to south – but side to side, not very wide, averaging only 300km (186 miles) from the Norwegian border to the Finnish border or the Baltic Sea.

Position: Sweden is the eastern half of the Scandinavian Peninsula, with a long border with Norway (to the west) and shorter one with Finland (to the east). The three countries meet at a point (Treriksröset) at Sweden's northern tip. In the south Sweden is just 4km (2.5 miles) from Denmark across Öresund.

Some numbers: Sweden's coastline measures about 7500km (4650 miles). The country has over 100,000 lakes. The Stockholm archipelago numbers over 25,000 islands. About 17% of the country lies north of the Arctic Circle.

the contrast, the folk who live here are also different: the Sámi reindeer herders' culture offers quite an unconventional take on life.

Taking it all together – marvellous scenery, exciting cities, history and culture – makes Sweden a marvellous place to visit.

THE LAND

Sweden is a long, narrow country. If the same length of journey from Sweden's most northerly town, **Kiruna**, to its most southerly, **Malmö**, were travelled southwards from London, the traveller would find himself somewhere between Rome and Naples. And there is more of Sweden north of Kiruna that cannot be reached by road (and a bit, but not much, south of Malmö too).

Geologically, Sweden forms a part of the **Baltic Shield** (or Fennoscandia), the nucleus of the European continent, with rocks more than 2000 million years old. The Caledonian folding of the post-Cambrian era of geological time pushed northern Europe against the rigid mass of the Baltic Shield creating the long ridge of mountains that now lies along the border of Norway and Sweden. Beyond this ridge the limestone that characterizes southern Sweden was laid down beneath a calm, shallow sea. All countries are defined by their geology, but in Sweden's case there was a later event that had a huge influence on the look of the country – the Ice Age. Sweden lies a long way north – Stockholm is on the

same latitude as southern Alaska and the northern end of Russia's Kamchatka Peninsula – and when the ice came it formed a sheet about 2km (1.25 miles) thick over the country, its weight causing a subsidence of around 700m (2300ft). The ice finished the erosion of the border mountains that aeons of

wind, rain and snow had
begun, but also etched the
peaks, creating the sharp
ridges that are now such a
feature of the scenery. The
ice, and its glacial tongues,
also created U-shaped
valleys and widened other
valleys. Most importantly
the glaciers ground up the

bedrock, producing a glacial till that was deposited
as moraine and left throughout the country as the ice
eventually retreated. That moraine is now a major
feature of Swedish geography.

Above: *Skåne is an area of water, trees and flowers.*
Opposite: *Sunset over Västmanland Lake.*

Geographically, Sweden is divided into two by the
Arctic Circle. Historically, the regions of **Svealand** (a
belt stretching west across the country from Stockholm)
and **Götaland** (in the southwest) united to form Sweden,
later wrestling the southeast of the country (comprising
Skåne, **Blekinge** and **Småland**) from the Danes.
These regions now form southern Sweden.

Southern Sweden

This is the part of the country in which most Swedes
live. In general the landscape is flat, rather similar to
Denmark which lies just across **Öresund**. Due to the
relatively low population density there are still large
areas of forest, but these are interspersed with farmland
and dotted with villages. Although urbanization has
occurred in Sweden as in other European countries,
there are still a very large number of villages and small
towns – a more visible memory of Sweden's agricultural
past than is seen elsewhere in Europe. Southern Sweden
also has a great number of lakes, including two vast
water masses, **Vänern** and **Vättern**. Because these lie
close to each other they have been utilized as part of the
Göta Canal which links the Skagerrak (part of the North
Sea) at **Gothenburg** to the Baltic Sea near Norrköping.
The coastline of southern Sweden is very varied. In
places, both on the west and east coasts, there are fjords,

MORE FACTS AND FIGURES

Longest river: Klarälven-
Göta River at 720km
(445 miles)
Largest lake: Vänern, in
southern Sweden, is the
largest lake in western
Europe with a surface area
of 5600km² (2200 sq. miles).
Largest island: Gotland is
also the largest in the Baltic
Sea. It covers an area of
3000km² (1200 sq. miles).
Population: 8.9 million. Of
these about 750,000 live in
Stockholm (though 1.5
million live in 'greater'
Stockholm) with a further
460,000 in Gothenburg
and 255,000 in Malmö. The
Swedes are an urban people,
over 80% of the population
living in towns of more than
500 people. By contrast, in
Lappland the population
density is as low as 3 people
per square kilometre.
Highest mountain:
Kebnekaise, 2111m (6926ft).

Above: *The Sarek is one of the world's great national parks and is justly popular with campers.*
Opposite: *Each year in Stockholm's Gamla Stan there is a festival of ice sculpture.*

some penetrating far inland. At other places, especially south of Gothenburg, there are excellent sandy beaches. On **Gotland**, Sweden's large Baltic island, there are also beautiful sea stacks, one of the highlights of a trip there.

Northern Sweden (Norrland)

Northern Sweden, that part of the country that lies north of Svealand, is much more than half the land area. It is characterized by an increasingly rugged terrain, mountains and wild empty valleys, and a decreasing population density. Immediately north of Svealand is a belt of metal-bearing rock which was the birthplace of Sweden's industrial revolution. At **Falun** the copper mine was the most important in the world for many years. At other places iron, lead, silver and even some gold have been worked, though here, as in most other parts of Europe, mining became increasingly uneconomical as larger ore deposits were found in parts of the world where labour was much cheaper. Iron ore deposits reappear at **Kiruna** where the mines were of extreme strategic importance during World War II.

Between the mining areas of Falun and Kiruna lies one of the last great wildernesses of Europe, though the coastal belt is a much more benign environment with a number of picturesque fishing villages whose inhabitants have been exploiting the riches of the Baltic Sea for centuries.

The National Parks

The Swedes are extremely environmentally conscious. This does not only mean that there are efficient sewage disposal systems and excellent recycling schemes, but that on a personal level the people are tidy and do not leave litter, even in towns and cities, in the way that has become the blight of other European countries. Not

---

THE AURORA BOREALIS

In the Arctic national parks – indeed, anywhere in Arctic Sweden – the visitor is likely to see the aurora borealis, or northern lights. The lights are caused by the interaction of charged particles from the sun with air molecules in the upper atmosphere. Normally the lights are green, but they can be red, and can move or shimmer.

surprisingly this environmental friendliness translated into a desire to protect pristine wilderness and in the early 20th century Sweden led the world in the creation of **national parks** and **nature reserves**. There are now more than two dozen national parks, and although the best-known are those that lie beyond the Arctic Circle, a significant number lie in southern Sweden. The Arctic parks vary in size from the tiny (**Vadvetjåkka** and **Abisko**, at less than 100km² or 40 sq. miles) to the vast (**Padjelanta** and **Sarek**, which, at almost 2000km² or about 800 sq. miles, are among the biggest in Europe). The Sarek is one of the finest national parks in the world, covering mountains, glaciers and rivers, birch and willow forests. It is not accessible by road, and visitors are required to walk in, or to take a boat in summer.

In the southern part of Norrland, Sweden's most recently created national park, **Färnebofjärden**, has been set up to protect an important bird site. In the south there are two island parks (**Blå Jungfrun** and **Gotska Sandön**), as well as fine inland parks: **Store Mosse**, near Värnamo, a marshland famous for its bird life, and **Stenshuvud**, on the southern coast near Simrishamn, noted for its cliff scenery and woodland.

Climate

Sweden is difficult to place in a single climatic category. The west coast is washed by the warm waters of the Gulf Stream, which produces cool, damp winters (and cool, damp summers) in northern Europe. Despite that, the landmasses of Norway and Jutland shield Sweden from the Atlantic weather systems so its annual rainfall is lower than that of neighbouring

SWEDISH FORESTS

Unlike the majority of European countries, the extent of forest cover in Sweden has been increasing over the last century. Forest now covers a little over 50% of the land area. Sustainable logging is likely to see this figure increased or maintained for the foreseeable future, a testament to Sweden's environmental credentials.

STOCKHOLM	J	F	M	A	M	J	J	A	S	O	N	D
MAX TEMP. °C	-1	-1	3	8	14	19	22	20	15	9	5	2
MIN TEMP. °C	-5	-5	-4	1	6	11	14	13	9	5	1	-2
MAX TEMP. °F	30	30	37	46	57	66	72	68	59	48	41	36
MIN TEMP. °F	23	23	25	40	43	52	57	55	48	41	40	28
HOURS OF SUN DAILY	4	5	6	8	9	11	12	12	9	7	5	4
RAINFALL mm	43	30	25	31	34	45	61	76	60	48	53	48
RAINFALL in.	1.1	0.9	0.8	0.9	1.2	1.8	2.8	2.6	2.3	2.2	1.6	1.4

NOTE: From Nov–May 'rainfall' can include snowfall. From Nov–Mar, snow is likely to exceed rain.

WIND CHILL

Work on the loss of heat by bodies with internal heat generation has led to the establishment of wind-chill figures. Wind chill is the apparent temperature experienced by bare flesh in a given wind speed.

Wind Speed		Air Temperature (°C)								
kph	mph	10	5	0	-5	-10	-15	-20	-25	-30
Still air		10	5	0	-5	-10	-15	-20	-25	-30
10	6	8	2	-2	-7	-12	-17	-23	-28	-33
20	12.5	5	0	-6	-11	-17	-23	-28	-34	-40
30	19	3	-2	-8	-14	-20	-26	-32	-38	-43
40	25	2	-4	-10	-17	-21	-29	-35	-41	-47
50	31	1	-6	-12	-19	-25	-32	-37	-44	-51
80	50	-2	-10	-17	-24	-31	-38	-45	-52	-59
100	62.5	-5	-13	-20	-27	-34	-43	-50	-57	-64

Norway. The downside of this is that most of the country is also shielded from the warming influence of the Atlantic. The east coast, particularly, is cold in winter, often very cold indeed. The Gulf of Bosnia freezes regularly. However, recent climatic changes (if real) may reduce the incidence of the biting cold that freezes the sea. In Sweden as elsewhere this good news will be tempered by the bad news of more unstable weather patterns and a greater frequency of extreme conditions.

Such water-laden air that does reach Sweden tends to drop its moisture on the western mountain ridge. In winter this produces excellent snow conditions which make Sweden a skiers' paradise, the cold and shortened days (in comparison to the European Alps) being compensated by guaranteed snow. In summer Sweden tends to be cooler than countries to the west, but stable air from Russia can mean long periods of dry, sunny weather when the temperature can rise to the high 20s. The long summer days are then delightful, filling the beaches of both the west and east coasts. Sea bathing is possible (and, indeed, prevalent), but it takes a hardier or more determined bather to enjoy the North or Baltic seas than is found on a Mediterranean beach.

The further north the visitor goes, the less the above statements apply. The Lappland summer is surprisingly benign, the extra long days seeing

Below: *Harebells in the Sarek National Park. Though renowned for its rugged wilderness, the Sarek is a gentler place in summer.*

temperatures which can, and frequently do, reach 20°C (68°F), and which occasionally go even higher. In winter Lappland is a harsher place. From October until April the temperature stays low, occasionally reaching -50°C (though rarely for long) and often staying below -10°C for long periods.

Flora and Fauna

From north to south, Sweden's plant life can be divided into a number of belts. In the extreme north there is an area of tundra, though this, and the mountain regions, are characterized more by alpine species than the pure Arctic tundra flora. The mountains are rich in wild flowers such as **saxifrages** and **gentians**, and contain patches of **dwarf birch**, **juniper** and **Arctic willow** above the tree line. Sheltered spots, and lower ground, also support a large number of edible berries including the **cloudberry** (*Rambus chamaemorus*). The amber-coloured cloudberries are a much sought after delicacy. On lower ground in Lappland and lying as a belt across the country to the south is coniferous forest, chiefly **Scots pine** and **Norway spruce**, but with various firs as well.

In 'central' Sweden the forest is more deciduous, with **birch** dominating but **alder** and **linden** occur as well. The forest floor is often covered with mosses and fungi, lichens proving the quality of the Swedish air. The forests, and the meadows beside them, support a wide variety of flowers, particularly where the soil is lime-based. On the islands of Gotland and Öland the lime-rich soil hosts several rare species including **orchids**.

To the south of the deciduous forest belt is another coniferous belt, though here the natural growth has been augmented by commercial forestry. Finally, in the south there is a belt of larger deciduous trees such as **beech** and **oak**.

Sweden's mammals include most European species as well as the northern animals – the chance of seeing which makes a journey to the Arctic national parks so exciting. Of these animals the **brown bear** is the prize sighting. The most elusive of the northern species is the

---

LEMMINGS

In a tale by James Thurber a man asks a talking lemming a question that has puzzled him for years – why do lemmings commit mass suicide? The lemming replies that, strangely, the question mirrors one of his own – why humans don't.

There are two species of lemming: the dark grey wood lemming which is a forest dweller, and the large orange and brown Norway lemming which inhabits Sweden's upland areas. It is the latter whose migrations have led to stories of mass suicide.

In 'lemming years' the population explodes and vast numbers of lemmings are forced to migrate in search of food. Faced with lakes they swim, often to their deaths if the lakes are large. Faced with cliffs, pressure of numbers forces those at the front to tumble over, apparently committing suicide.

Above: *Less elusive than the other Arctic wildlife species, reindeer are also among the most popular of Sweden's animals. Only female reindeer retain their antlers during the early winter.*

lynx, Europe's largest wild cat. Equally elusive, but due to the fact that persecution has drastically reduced their numbers, are the wolf and wolverine. Now banned, but once officially sanctioned, killing and, more recently, illegal hunting by farmers have reduced the Swedish **wolf** population to below 100. Attempts to increase numbers meet with hostile reactions from locals and, though the population is stable, the animal's future is uncertain. The **wolverine**, an extremely elusive member of the badger family, was hunted (and is now poached) for its fur. The population (probably 200–300) is now thought to be increasing.

Of other large animals visitors to northern Sweden will certainly see reindeer, and it is possible (but unlikely) to spot an **elk** almost anywhere – they cross the road, as the 'Beware of the elk' signs indicate. Elk (moose in America) are the world's largest deer.

Sweden is as good for northern bird species as it is for Arctic mammals, but its forests, coasts, and the flatter, more pastoral country of the south mean that it also supports many other uncommon species. In the north **rough-legged buzzards** and the much rarer **gyrfalcon** are Arctic species. The mountains are home to **golden eagles**, while **white-tailed sea eagles** breed on the coast.

Sweden's forests are inhabited by **goshawks**, and also by the beautiful **waxwings**, particularly in winter when they arrive from Russia. In the south, the woods are also the place to see the colourful **golden oriole**. On the lakes there are numerous duck and goose species, as well as less common species such as **black- and red- throated divers** and **Slovenian grebes**. Waders include **bitterns**, three species of **sandpiper** and the **black-tailed godwit**. On the coast the lucky visitor may spot a **little gull** or a **Caspian tern**.

OWLS

As well as long- and short-eared, hawk, tawny, Tengmalm's and pygmy, Sweden is home to the largest of European owls – the great grey, the Ural, the eagle and the snowy. All are desirable sightings for the bird-watcher, but for most it is the white, day-flying snowy owl that is the prize. Its population follows that of the lemming (*see* panel, page 11), rising sharply in 'lemming years' and crashing when the rodents are scarce.

HISTORICAL CALENDAR

ca. 8000BC Man reaches Sweden from the south (the ancestors of the Swedes), and also from Asia (the ancestors of the Sámi).

ca. 2000BC Man leaves his first known mark on the Swedish landscape.

500AD Migration of proto-Vikings into southern Sweden.

400–800 Rise of the Svea on Mälaren.

793 The Viking Age. Swedish Vikings head east rather than west with their Danish and Norwegian cousins.

9th century First attempts to convert the Swedes to Christianity. Sweden does not finally convert until the 12th century.

ca. 1250 Birger Jarl founds Stockholm.

1319 Norway and Sweden are united.

1350 Black Death kills one-third of Swedes.

1397 The Kalmar Union unites Denmark, Norway and Sweden under a common crown.

1520 The Stockholm Bloodbath.

1523 Kalmar Union dissolved; Gustav Vasa becomes King of Sweden. Norway remains united with Denmark.

1527 Church property seized. Gustav Vasa introduces Reformation. Lutheran Church becomes dominant.

1657–8 After a century of war with Denmark, Sweden finally defeats the Danes and regains all Danish territory in Sweden.

1660 Rebellion on Bornholm returns the island to Denmark.

1718 Sweden invades Norway. Expedition ends when King Karl XII is assassinated.

18th century Age of Enlightenment. Work of Linnaeus, Celsius and others in science.

1792 Assassination of King Gustav III.

1808 Russia invades Finland.

1809 King Gustav IV abdicates.

1814 Sweden gains Norway from Denmark as a result of the Napoleonic Wars.

19th century Industrialization. Falun copper mine exploited. Göta Canal built.

1905 Norway achieves independence.

1914–18 World War I. Sweden remains neutral, but British blockade cripples economy. Sweden loses Åland to Finland.

1939–45 World War II. Sweden remains neutral, but allows German troop movement to ensure its neutrality.

1974 Abba win Eurovision Song Contest with *Waterloo*.

1986 Assassination of Olof Palme.

1995 Sweden joins the European Union.

2000 Öresund bridge links Sweden and Denmark.

HISTORY IN BRIEF

It is possible that Sweden was visited, perhaps even settled, as long as 80,000 years ago during the interglacial periods of the last Ice Age. Permanent settlement did not appear until about 10,000 years ago when the Ice Age ended. Then hunter-gatherers following the ice northwards arrived from central Europe, while the ancestors of the Sámi migrated west from northern central Asia. These first Swedes were Palaeolithic, Old-Stone-Age folk who lived a predominantly nomadic life. Much later,

Below: *Cup marks on a boulder near Malmö's castle. The strange marks were made by Sweden's earliest dwellers.*

ALES STENAR

The name of this magnificent site is not well understood. *Stenar* definitely means stones but *Ales* could mean a ridge or a temple. What it is almost certainly not is the name of a man. The site comprises 58 stones arranged in the shape of a ship 67m (73yd) long and 19m (21yd) wide. The tallest stone – 3.3m (10ft) high – is at the stern. The ship is aligned towards the midsummer sunset and midwinter sunrise.

during the Neolithic, New Stone Age, the people built permanent dwellings and buried their dead in *gångrift* (dolmen), the characteristic tomb consisting of upright stone slabs capped by another slab to form a box. Sometimes a passage of slabs would lead to the tomb, creating a passage grave. One of the best examples of the form is to be seen at **Ekornavallen**, near Falköping in Götaland, which has been dated to about 2000BC.

The Bronze and Iron Ages

The Stone-Age builders of the Ekornavallen grave were eventually replaced by the Bronze-Age culture. Despite Sweden's richness of metal ore-bearing rocks, bronze was not easily obtained in the country. Most bronze objects were imported from central Europe, the cost probably explaining why so few metal items have been discovered from this period. What does remain is a large number of rock carvings portraying hunting scenes, animals, boats and the sun. Of these, some of the best can be seen near **Norrköping** where the works even include a representation of a cart pulled by an animal, complete with a carter. The Bronze-Age folk buried their dead in round mounds, the site at **Kivik**, a village near Kristianstad, being the most important of all Swedish sites. Here the burial was in a 'box' of eight engraved slabs beneath a shield-shaped mound measuring 75m (82yd) across its long side.

With the coming of the Iron Age the burial of chieftains changed from the mound of Kivikgraven to a form that suggests the people who have become the most famous of Scandinavians. At **Ales Stenar**, the fabulous

Below: *Sweden has some of the finest prehistoric rock carvings in Europe. Known as* hällristningar, *they often depict animals and boats.*

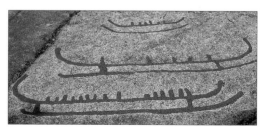

upright stones close to the sea east of Ystad in southern Sweden, the stones form the shape of a ship. Such ship settings are actually common in Sweden, particularly from the later Viking era, and point to the development of a ship-based culture.

The Vikings

During the period between the 4th and 7th centuries there seem to have been migrations into southern Sweden and conflict between tribal groups which led to the supremacy in the area around the Mälaren Lake – then connected by an easily navigable waterway

to the Baltic Sea – of the **Svea**. To the southwest another tribe, the **Gauts**, were rising to prominence. The Svea were proto-Vikings, their ship-based economy (with trade and probable piracy across the northern Baltic) being aided by the safe anchorage of Mälaren. In the mid-8th century the Svea founded the town of **Birka** on Björkö, an island in Mälaren – the first town in Sweden. From this town, which had about 1000 people at the height of its importance, the Svea kings ruled their *rike* (kingdom). This kingdom – *Svearike* – was to give its name to the country: Sverige.

The Viking Age is usually said to have begun with the raid in June 793 on the monastery of Lindisfarne on England's northeast coast. The rich but poorly defended churches and monasteries of Britain were easy targets, but Vikings ranged much further afield. They raided French monasteries and towns; a Frankish monk writing at Noirmoutier, an island off Brittany's extreme southern coast, in the 860s notes 'The number of ships grow: the endless stream of Vikings knows no end. Everywhere Christians are victims of massacres, fire, plunderings: the Vikings overwhelm all in their path and no one can stand against them.' The writer goes on to note that 'Bordeaux, Toulouse, Tours, Orleans have been destroyed, Rouen laid waste, Paris captured, Chartres captured and Bayeux plundered'. The monk runs out of words to describe the annihilation long before he runs out of towns. The Vikings also ranged much further than

Above: *The reconstructed Viking fortress at Trelleborg in southern Sweden.*

VIKING

The Vikings are synonymous with Scandinavia, but it is worth noting that the origin of the word in unclear. *Vik* is the Old Norse word for a bay, a place where a long-boat could be safely moored. But it also seems that the Old Norse word for a pirate was *viking*, so perhaps the first Viking raiders preyed upon their own countryfolk. The Vikings were seafarers, the longboats that terrorized half of Europe starting as ships that tamed the tricky waters of the Baltic, the Kattegatt and Skagerrak – fast and highly manoeuvrable ships powered either by a single sail or rowed by pairs of oars.

Above: *Birger Jarl, the founder of Stockholm, is commemorated in a statue on Riddarholmen.*

France and England, raiding Lisbon, Cadiz, Seville several towns on Africa's Mediterranean coast, and reaching Italy where they pillaged Pisa. Crossing the Atlantic they settled Iceland and Greenland, and reached the coast of North America. Though Swedes probably joined the Norse (Norwegians) and Danes in these journeys of plunder and exploration, it seems that most stayed at home farming and trading.

In the early 9th century St Ansgar, a Benedictine monk, arrived to attempt to convert the inhabitants of Birka. He built a church, but failed in his mission, and the town remained pagan (though with some Christian converts) until the 10th century when it was supplemented as the Svea's main centre by **Sigtuna**. The new centre was pagan too; Christianity did not finally replace the Viking pantheon of gods until the 12th century. By then the Svea had overcome the Gauts of the south, uniting the two into a Swedish state. In 1160 the king of this new country, **Erik Jedvarsson**, established a Christian state of which, as St Erik, he is now the patron saint. Following Erik's assassination in Uppsala in 1160 his son, Knut, assumed the throne. When Knut died in 1196 civil war ensued and a council of ministers, Jarls, eventually took power. Under the greatest of those, **Birger Jarl**, Sweden expanded north and east, taking Finland but being stopped by the Russians near St Petersburg in 1240. At around the same time the rise in land levels made the water journey from the Baltic to Mälaren increasingly difficult, resulting in Birger Jarl's **founding of Stockholm**. With Birger Jarl's death hereditary kingship returned, and his son Magnus Ladulås assumed power. He was a strong leader and the stability he brought allowed such ventures as the building of Uppsala Cathedral. But Magnus' son, though given his grandfather's name, Birger, was a cruel, poor ruler. He starved his brothers to death and was eventually exiled

---

NAME THAT DAY

The Danish influence on England (and, consequently, the English-speaking world) can be seen in the days of the week, several of which are named for the Viking pantheon. The supreme god was Odin, or Wodin, for whom Wednesday is named. Odin was married to Frigga who named Friday. Their son was Thor, god of thunder (but also of agriculture). Thursday is named for him, while Tuesday is named for Tyr, or Tow, the god of war.

to Denmark, his departure leading to chaos which ended only with the unification of Norway and Sweden. Then, in 1350, Black Death killed around one-third of the population leaving Sweden in a parlous position.

The Kalmar Union

Southwestern Sweden was under Danish rule and the Hanseatic League had taken Visby (and therefore Gotland). Ultimately the threat of the League persuaded Sweden of the benefits of a Scandinavian alliance and in 1397 the **Kalmar Union**, sealed at Kalmar Castle, united Denmark, Norway and Sweden. At first, under the direction of the Danish regent Margrethe and then her nephew Erik of Pomerania, the Union helped Sweden, but gradually the country grew to resent the dominance of Denmark, particularly when the Danes attacked the country to quell growing nationalism. A Swedish army under **Sten Sture** defeated the Danes in 1471, but that did not curb Danish aggression This culminated in the **Stockholm Bloodbath** of 1520: Sten Sture's son was one of those beheaded. Before 1520 the nobleman **Gustav Vasa** had tried, but failed, to incite an uprising. The Bloodbath gave him what he needed to arouse an ambivalent nation and he drove the Danes out. The Kalmar Union was dissolved in 1523 and Gustav became the first king of the Vasa dynasty. The reign of Gustav Vasa was also notable for the Swedish Reformation, Lutheran Protestants taking religious control of the country, a position they maintain.

Over the next century Denmark and Sweden fought a series of campaigns as the Danes tried to regain control of mainland Scandinavia. At the same time Sweden extended its empire on the eastern side of the Baltic, taking Latvia and invading Poland.

THE WARRIOR KING

King Gustav II Adolf came to the throne in 1611 at the age of 17. Despite his youth he was a military genius who rapidly pushed the Danes out of much of southern Sweden and then began a 30-year war with Poland and the German states in support of the Protestants. Using money from the Falun copper mine he moulded an army of farm labourers into a formidable fighting force, reaching Bavaria. Gustav was killed in 1632 fighting the Catholic Hapsburg army at the Battle of Lützen.

Below: *Kalmar Castle in Skåne, where the Union between the Scandinavian kingdoms was forged.*

Opposite: *On its way
from the Skagerrak to the
Baltic the Göta Canal
passes through Gothenburg.*

THE KING'S ASSASSINATION

King Gustav III was greatly
influenced by French culture
and the new Renaissance,
and under him Swedish
science flourished. But he
was an absolute monarch
and felt able to involve the
country in a costly war with
Russia without consultation
with his nobles. In 1792 he
was shot by one of these
nobles, Capt Anckarström, at
a masked ball at Stockholm's
Opera House. The king died
14 days later. Anckarström
was publicly flogged on three
successive days before being
executed. The murder was
the basis of Verdi's opera
Un Ballo in Maschera.

Below: *The rune stone
erected at Rättvik in 1893 to
commemorate Gustav Vasa.*

Then in 1657–8, a winter claimed to be one of the
coldest in Denmark's history, Sweden invaded Denmark
across the frozen Kattegatt, forcing the Danes to sign the
Treaty of Roskilde which gave all Danish territory in
southern Sweden to the Swedish crown. (The Swedes
also received Bornholm, but a local rebellion in 1660
ousted them, returning the island to Danish control.)
The Swedish empire was now at its greatest extent, but
it was not to last. The Russians took the Baltic States
and Finland, though that did not entirely stop Sweden's
imperialist ambitions. In 1716 Sweden invaded Norway
taking Christiania (as Oslo was then called) and laying
siege to Trondheim. Then during the winter of 1718–19
King Karl XII was shot dead in mysterious circumstances
and the invasion ended.

The Age of Enlightenment

In the 18th century, Sweden reflected the Age of
Enlightenment, particularly in the sciences with the
work of **Linnaeus** in botany, **Scheele** in chemistry and
Celsius in physics. The Swedish Academies of Science
and Literature were founded and the Swedish parliament (*riksdag*), passed the world's first Freedom of the
Press Act. Despite this, Swedish colonial ambitions were
not entirely ended. Finland had been retaken, lost and
taken again. Ultimately Sweden was drawn into a two-

year war with Russia
which ended with King
Gustav III being assassinated. His son, Gustav IV,
declared war on France
during the Napoleonic
Wars, a decision that owed
more to macho posturing
than common sense. In
1808 Russia invaded
Finland yet again and
Sweden was forced to
sign a treaty renouncing
its claim to the country.

Gustav abdicated and a new constitution limited royal powers. Yet despite this move towards democracy Sweden continued to enforce its union with Norway, the latter not achieving independence until 1905.

Modern Sweden

By the time of Norwegian independence Sweden was an industrial state, the metal ores of the central belt transforming the country and, together with timber, Alfred Nobel's dynamite and the invention of the safety match, increasing its export earnings. The opening of the Göta Canal helped wealth production and the Swedish parliament introduced a series of social reforms that paved the way to a modern welfare state. After the 'loss' of Norway, Swedish antipathy towards costly military adventurism led to a neutral stance in World War I. Britain (correctly) detected pro-German sympathies in Sweden's neutrality and demanded a cessation of trade with Germany. When this did not materialize Swedish goods were blacklisted and its ships pirated, a situation which crippled Sweden's economy. The Russian revolution in 1917 added to Swedish woes. Finland fought for independence from the new Russia and, despite assistance by some Swedish volunteers, annexed Åland. The islanders objected, wishing to remain Swedish, but were overruled by the League of Nations. The island remains Finnish (and, consequently, offers an easy duty-free trip for Swedes).

Sweden maintained its neutral stance during World War II but took the pragmatic view that allowing German troop movements through the north of the country would be better than blocking them and risking occupation. In the postwar era Sweden's reputation for

RAOUL WALLENBERG

Raoul Wallenberg was born in 1912 and at the outbreak of World War II was a diplomat in the Swedish Embassy in Budapest. Sweden remained neutral during the war and, using Swedish passports, Wallenberg helped many Hungarian Jews to escape the Nazi concentration camps. In 1945 when the Soviet army liberated Budapest he was taken to Moscow where he is said to have died in Lubyanka Prison. However, there have been persistent rumours that he was alive well after this, the Soviets, and now the Russians, being unable or unwilling to provide concrete evidence of his death, to satisfactorily discount the stories or to explain why he was imprisoned in the first place.

independence of creation and quality of production was reinforced by the successes of Volvo and Saab (and by the equal successes in the fields of sport and culture – Björn Borg, Ingmar Bergman, Abba). With the Social Democrats in power a welfare state was introduced that protected citizens from the worst excesses of unbridled capitalism. This was the envy of many other countries, but inevitably a concern for others and may have contributed to the assassination of Prime Minister Olof Palme in 1986, an event which shook Swedish confidence to its roots. It is interesting to speculate whether the pre-86 Sweden would have voted in favour of joining the European Union (EU) in 1995. Certainly, present concerns over the widening gap between rich and poor and the cracks appearing in the social cohesion that was the hallmark of Sweden's democracy are causing many Swedes to question the value of EU membership. The decision not to join the Euro Zone (the Euro is the single currency of the EU) for the present was seen by many as a return to Swedish neutrality (and, perhaps, a vote of no confidence in the EU) and it will be interesting to see how the vote goes in the promised referendum.

THE ASSASSINATION OF OLOF PALME

On 28 February 1986 Olof Palme (born 1927) was murdered at the corner of Sveavägen and Tunnelgatan in Stockholm as he was walking home from the cinema. It was typical of both Sweden and the man that Palme was walking, and that he had no bodyguard. The killing remains an unsolved crime. Palme was famous for his outspoken views on foreign dictators, on social democracy, Third World debt and the arms race, none of which made him popular abroad. Sweden's welfare state was also viewed with suspicion by some. Conspiracy theories abound, but today the general view is that there was foreign involvement, the aims being to silence Palme and destabilize Sweden. Both aims were certainly accomplished.

GOVERNMENT AND ECONOMY

Sweden is a constitutional monarchy. The monarchy is hereditary, the monarch being Head of State, but having no direct role in government. The present monarch is King Carl XVI Gustaf (born in 1946, came to the throne in 1973) whose wife is Queen Silvia. Their eldest daughter, Princess Victoria, is heir to the throne.

The Swedish government is democratically elected at general elections (and by-elections as necessary) every four years. The parliament (*riksdag*) has 349 seats. The voting system is proportional representation, any party gaining more than 4% of the popular vote being guaranteed a seat. All citizens over 18 years of age may vote. The prime minister is called the *statsminister* and he/she chooses the cabinet (*regeringen*). Presently, the left-of-centre Social Democrats – the largest party, but with no overall majority – head a coalition government with the Left and Green parties. Sweden is a member of the European Union, but maintains the neutrality it exhibited during the two World Wars and so is not a member of NATO.

Historically Swedish governments have been left-of-centre and liberal, promoting social welfare and attempting to follow midway between rampant capitalism and outright socialism (but not communism). Recently, as elsewhere in Europe, there has been a rise in support for extreme right-wing politics (Sweden has a large immigrant population and, therefore, a ready-made target) and, as a reaction, increased support for extreme left parties. It remains to be seen whether the mild left/centre/liberal alliance can maintain power.

> **THE NATIONAL FLAG**
>
> Sweden's flag was adopted on 22 June 1906 though its design was by then several hundred years old. It was certainly in use by the 16th century and flew from the *Vasa* when it sank in 1628. The colours derive from the Swedish national arms (again as depicted on the *Vasa*) though the design was taken from the Danish flag.

The Economy

Historically Sweden's economy depended on its exports of iron and timber. This is still true to an extent though the ore mines of Kiruna and southern Norrland are no longer as critical as they once were. Forestry is still a major export source, both timber and timber products (pulp and paper) being significant markets. Lately to these have been added the export of timber as ready-packed furniture by the **IKEA** company. Formed in the aftermath

Opposite: *A tram in Kungsportsavenyn at the heart of Gothenburg.*
Below: *The Swedes are very proud of their flag and display it at every opportunity. This one is on a boat in Kalmar's harbour.*

NUCLEAR POWER

Sweden is the only country to have held a referendum (in 1980) on the closing of its nuclear power stations, the population voting in favour because of environmental concerns. These concerns were reinforced by the effects of fallout from the Chernobyl accident of 1986. However, later pragmatism has revised the proposed closure programme. Sweden has great potential for hydro-power, but existing schemes have proved anything but environmentally friendly, with damage to fish stocks, scarring of the land and displacement of people. If nuclear power (which produces around 40% of Swedish electricity) is phased out, what will replace it? With present concerns over carbon dioxide emissions, the suggestion of fossil-fuel power stations does not seem to be an acceptable solution.

of World War II, the company initially had just two outlets (one north, the other south, of Stockholm) but now has megastores in many western countries. The company has brought the Swedish love of wood – and Scandinavian design ideals – to a wider world.

The Swedes were also famous for the production of motor cars. For so small a nation – in population terms – the existence of two independent companies, **Volvo** and **Saab**, was remarkable in an age of mass production. In both cases the companies competed against volume manufacturers by producing cars at the executive end of the market. Saab coupled this with the production of aircraft, equipping the Swedish Air Force with home-produced planes. The cars produced by Sweden (Volvo especially, though Saab was not immune) were criticized in other countries – Volvos, it was said, were agricultural vehicles, more like tractors than cars – but the comments invariably stemmed from a sneaking admiration and jealousy. When Volvo and Saab were taken over by the US giants (Ford and General Motors respectively) in 1999 the sense of loss in Sweden was palpable.

As well as cars Sweden also produces pharma-ceuticals (the Astra companies), telecommunications equipment companies (Ericsson), and armaments (Bofors). The impact on the Swedish economy of such things as pop music should also not be underestimated.

It is claimed that in the last years of the 1970s only Volvo exceeded Abba in terms of foreign income to the country.

THE PEOPLE

There are two indigenous races in Sweden. The ancestors of the people in the south are those who moved north after the last Ice Age. These **Nordic** people are tall, fair-haired and blue-eyed, the folk-loric Swedish blondes – though there are dark Nordic people as well. In the north of the country are the **Sámi**, a much shorter and darker folk whose ancestors came from the Asiatic steppes many thousands of years ago. It is known from the Viking sagas that there was contact and trade between the southerners

Above: *Tradition lives on in Sweden's mid-summer celebrations.*
Opposite: *Changing of the Royal Guard in Gamla Stan.*

and the Sámi, though it is unlikely to have been more than spasmodic until proto-Viking times. When, later, the Swedes moved north they discovered that Sámi methods were best suited to living in the north and integration was to the Sámi way of life. As a general rule there has been little movement of Sámi southwards, the old life still being seen as best. With help from the Swedish parliament (*riksdag*), a Sámi parliament (*Sámiting*) has been established to look after the interests of the Sámi, but displacement for hydroelectric schemes, disruption caused by mining and other attacks on the old ways suggest that the parliament has been less than effective. The Sámi speak one of four dialects of a tongue common across Norway, Sweden, Finland and north-western Russia (in the latter two countries five further distinctive dialects are recognized).

There are also a large number (several hundred thousand) of Finns in Sweden. As Finland and Sweden were once united many Finns have Swedish ancestry and speak Swedish (as do many Finns in Finland). There are, though, 35,000 or so Finnish speakers in the country. Sweden also has Norwegians and Danes resident in the country and, historically, has had one of the highest immigration rates per capita from outside Europe of any European nation. More recently this immigration has been much more tightly controlled.

THE VIKING LANGUAGE

The Swedes speak a lan-guage which is Germanic in origin and which is almost identical to that spoken in Norway and Denmark. Danes, Norwegians and Sweden can understand each other when talking their own languages, the differences being effectively dialectic in the way that other countries have regional dialects. The three languages have their common origin in the Viking tongue. Icelanders, who were isolated from Scandinavia for centuries, speak a language almost identical to the original and cannot under-stand, or be understood by, their mainland cousins.

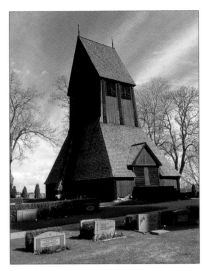

Above: *The church at Gamla Uppsala stands on an ancient pagan site.*

RELIGION

Most Swedes with religious convictions are members of the Lutheran Protestant Church of Sweden. Officially around 85% of the population are members. Of the remaining Christians most are members of non-conformist faiths or of the Finnish and Russian Orthodox churches. There are also many Roman Catholics. Sweden has about 250,000 Muslims and 20,000 Jews. The Sámi have embraced Christianity, and there seems to be no trace of the original Shamanistic practices.

The Social Swede

A famous tale claims to define the character of the Nordic races in a nutshell. Two men from each of the five Nordic states find themselves marooned on the proverbial desert island. At the end of the first week the two Danes have written a constitution and have the framework for an island council. The Finns have felled trees, some for firewood, some for the Norwegians to construct a boat from which to fish for food. At night the Icelanders, who have helped with the fishing, keep the group entertained with tales of the Viking heroes. By contrast the Swedes have done nothing, being unable to co-operate as no one has introduced them to each other.

The story has a kernel of truth in that the Swedes are, at first, a formal people and, at all times, serious-minded. It is not a surprise that on many occasions Sweden has been the conscience of the world. Though deeply proud of their nation, on closer inspection you will discover that whereas the French are proud of being French (an attribute they share with the British and Americans), the Swedes are proud of Sweden rather than of being Swedish. It is the land, its lakes and forest, its natural beauty, which attracts them. They are also proud of their egalitarianism, being suspicious of those who get above themselves by becoming rich or famous. Another characteristic is *svårmod*, a melancholia which derives, it seems, from the long, dark winters which, though producing a hardy folk, also induce a sadness that borders on depression (and has been identified as a significant cause of Scandinavian suicides).

Perhaps the joy of the returning sun explains the Swedish enthusiasm for parties; Walpurgis Night (the eve of 1 May) is celebrated with great enthusiasm throughout Sweden. Though named for an 8th-century English nun, Walpurgis is also associated with the witches' Sabbath. Such a pagan origin implies a similarity with other May Day festivities throughout northern Europe which are seen as celebrating the returning sun.

By contrast, the Sámi are fun-loving people given to simple pleasures and with an attitude to life which is totally pragmatic. Their craftwork shows that the Sámi are not blind to the beauty of art, but their approach to life is rational, an approach based on generations of life in a hard, unforgiving landscape.

The Arts

Sweden's greatest contribution to the advancement of civilization has been in the arts. **August Strindberg** (1849–1912) was born in Stockholm, the son of a steamship agent and a waitress. His mother died when he was 13, her death leaving a legacy of unhappiness which touched much of his work. He studied theology and medicine at Uppsala University, but did not complete either course. He then worked as a librarian and journalist until success as a writer came with the publication of *The Red Room* in 1884. His short story collection *Marriage* saw him tried (but acquitted) for blasphemy, and later radical works brought him into conflict with the establishment, his private life, involving three divorces, not helping his standing. He was, however, admired by the 'ordinary' people who funded

ALLEMANSRÄTTEN

Allemansrätten translates as 'every man's right' and encapsulates the Swedes' feeling for their country. It is an unwritten right of access which permits the Swedes to hunt and fish, and to walk and camp for one night anywhere, provided they do no damage, do not fell live trees or allow fires to get out of control. Over time these absolute rights have been restricted to accept the need for regulation in a civilized society. Hunting is regulated, fishing requires permits (except on the coast and in the largest lakes), and camping is not allowed on obviously private land. Otherwise *allemansrätten* still applies.

Left: *August Strindberg wrote* Inferno *in Lund, as this plaque notes.*

OTHER WRITERS

Other writers who are known
to an international audience
include **Carl Michael
Bellman**, the 18th-century
ballad writer and author of
Fredman's Epistles, a series
of stories based on classic
themes, and **Göran Sonnevi**
(born in 1939) whose poetry
was influential during the
Vietnam War.

an anti-Nobel prize for him when the real prize
was not awarded. Strindberg died of cancer, still
unrecognized by the Swedish Academy.

By contrast **Selma Lagerlöf** (1858–1940), despite
her own opposition to the establishment, did receive
the Nobel Prize for Literature, in 1909, the first of five
Swedish writers who have been so honoured. Lagerlöf's
best-known works are *The Wonderful Adventures of Nils*
and *The Saga of Gösta Berling*, each of which has been
translated into dozens of languages. Their superb
characterizations make them continuingly loved by
the Swedes. A third writer of international repute is
Astrid Lindgren (1907–2002) whose Pippi Longstocking
stories have delighted millions of children.

In fine art the most famous Swede is sculptor **Carl
Milles** (1875–1955). Born in Uppsala, Milles studied in
Paris where he was influenced by the work of Rodin.
Many of his works can be seen at his old home near
Stockholm. In 1930 Milles left Sweden for the USA
where he became an American citizen. Of painters,
the most famous are **Anders Zorn** and **Carl Larsson**.

In classical music, Sweden's contribution has been
limited. **Jenny Lind** (1820–1997) was an international
opera star. Known as the 'Swedish nightingale' she was
the (unconsummated) love of Hans Christian Andersen
(who wrote *The Nightingale* in her honour). In the field
of popular music **Abba** – Agnetha, Björn, Benny and

Opposite: *A memorial to
Tycho Brahe at Helsing-
borg, close to his observatory on the island of Hven.*
Right: *The museum to the
work of Anders Zorn in his
old house at Mora.*

Anni-Frid – are one of the best-selling groups in pop history. Beginning with their 1974 Eurovision Song Contest winner *Waterloo* Abba had a string of hit singles. The two men have continued as the writers of musicals, but the female members have been much less assured since the group broke up. Today the **Cardigans** and **Roxette** carry the flag for Swedish pop.

In cinema Swedes have excelled both in front of and behind the camera. Greta Gustafsson, born in Stockholm in 1905, achieved fame as **Greta Garbo**, one of the great faces of 1920s and 30s cinema before, famously, retiring to escape the system. She died in 1990. **Ingrid Bergman** (1916–1982) will for ever be famous as the beautiful star of *Casablanca*, but made other excellent films and received three Oscars. Her namesake, **Ingmar Bergman** (born 1918) spent years as a director of Swedish theatre before achieving world renown as a film director.

The Scientists

Tycho Brahe, the astronomer, was Swedish-born, though at that time the country was under Danish rule. Brahe had an observatory on the island of Ven, off Helsingborg. The most famous of Swedish scientists is undoubtedly **Carl von Linné** (Carolus Linnaeus), 1707–78, whose scientific naming system for plants and animals is still in use today. Linnaeus was active at Uppsala where **Anders Celsius** (1701–44) also worked. Celsius, a mathematician and astronomer, is famous for the temperature scale that bears his name. Another Uppsala scientist was **Carl Scheele** (1742–86), a chemist who discovered chlorine and prepared oxygen before Priestley. Scheele also made other important discoveries in the field of chemical compounds. As an inventor, **Nils Gustav Dalén**

FANNY AND ALEXANDER

Ingmar Bergman's most famous film was the Oscar-winning *Fanny and Alexander* released 20 years ago. It was also his last film, as he returned to work in theatre and TV in Sweden. He now lives on Faro, although he maintains an apartment in Stockholm. In December 2003 nearly a million Swedes watched *Salabad* – his latest, made for television, film. This is expected to go on general release.

(1869–1937) was world-class, particularly in the field of automatic marine beacons, inventing the system where the duration of light pulses identified the source. He was awarded the Nobel Prize for Physics in 1912.

The Nobel Prize

Though born in Bernhard, **Alfred Nobel** (1833–1896) spent much of his childhood in St Petersburg where his father (Immanuel) had an explosives factory. Alfred studied chemistry in Paris and worked with John Ericsson in the USA, then returned to Sweden to work on nitroglycerine with his father. In 1863 he invented the Nobel patent detonator which generated a shock wave, rather than heat, to detonate the main charge. The detonator revolutionized blasting. Sadly his attempt to mass produce the very unstable nitroglycerine – on an old farm called Heleneborg, in Stockholm – ended in an explosion which killed five people including his younger brother Emil. Forbidden by the government to reopen the works, Nobel experimented on a barge in Vinterviken (Winter Creek) on Mälaren, discovering, by chance, that *kieselguhr* (a porous siliceous earth) absorbed huge quantities of nitroglycerine and that the result, which Nobel called dynamite, was stable. Nobel rather naively thought that more powerful explosives would make war less, not more, likely. He did not marry and used the huge fortune dynamite made him to create a foundation to give prizes for advances in physics, chemistry, physiology/medicine, literature and peace. These have been awarded every year since 1901. In 1968 the Bank of Sweden added a sixth prize, for economics.

Food and Drink

The most typical of Swedish dishes is *smörgåsbord*, a buffet which normally starts with herring in a variety of forms (smoked, pickled, marinated, served with raw onion or mustard sauce) followed by a cold table, probably *gravadlax* (salmon marinated for 48 hours or so in salt and sugar), served with potatoes with dill, and then a selection of hot plates. The hot plates might include meat stews or meatballs, served with a variety of vegetables. The meal will be accompanied by bread, the dark rye bread which is very popular, the thin barley crispbread which was seen in other European countries a few years ago but is now less fashionable, or *knåckebrod*, a hard bread of wheat and/or rye which is an acquired taste.

Baltic salmon is very popular, not only cold as *gravadlax*, smoked or salted, but also as a steak which can be grilled, fried or poached. Meat is also very much in evidence. The Swedes enjoy pork, very popular dishes being *falukorv* – a pork sausage, boiled or fried – and *rotmos och fläskkorv* – a mix of pork sausage and root vegetables, chiefly turnip, that is guaranteed to ward off winter's chills. Sweden also offers more exotic meats such as reindeer and elk. Reindeer is superb, particularly as a steak served with lingonberry, or smoked and served cold. Elk has a subtler flavour, but is equally good.

Coffee is the popular after-meal drink, the standard preparations – latte, cappuccino, etc. – being available. Alcoholic drinks are expensive – the sale of alcohol outside bars and restaurants is controlled by the state – but the full range of beers, spirits and wines is available.

DESSERTS

Desserts tend to be similar to those eaten across Europe, but some local specialities do exist – **rose hip 'soup'**, sometimes served hot, but more often cold with ice cream, and **cloudberries**, a delicacy which takes Swedes (and their Norwegian cousins) into the mountains in search of the elusive, highly sought-after amber-coloured berries.

Below: *Pavement cafés are more popular than might be imagined: this one is on Gotland.*

2
Stockholm

Without having seen every nation's capital it is difficult to be certain that, as is often written, Stockholm is the most beautiful capital city in the world. But this is a city with the vibrancy of London, with the elegance and sophistication of Paris, with buildings every bit as impressive as those of Vienna, and with waterways that would do justice to Amsterdam and Venice. If it is not indeed the most beautiful in the world then it is a strong contender for the title. And, as well as being visually stunning, Stockholm is historically interesting. While it may not have as long a pedigree as Rome, or have been the centre of as influential an empire as Rome was, its Viking legacy is an important one, one too often overlooked.

THE HISTORY OF STOCKHOLM

The founding of Stockholm is slightly mysterious. The Icelandic saga writer Snorri Sturluson, writing in the early 13th century, refers to the existence of an island formed by the piling of tree trunks at a site close to what is now Norrström and a defensive tower which had stood for over a hundred years. As Lake Mälaren was used as a safe haven for the ships of the Svea, such defences are not unreasonable. It is also known that a rise in land levels caused the easily navigable passage between Mälaren and the Baltic to become more difficult, and that in about 1250 Birger Jarl, the chief of the Svea and therefore the most powerful man in the country, founded a new town closer to the Baltic, one he pro-

DON'T MISS

*** Vasamuseet: surely the most remarkable historical find in Europe?
*** Gamla Stan: the oldest part of Stockholm, with tight, atmospheric streets.
** Historiska Museet: astonishing treasures, including the stunning Gold Room.
** Kungliga Slottet: Stockholm's Royal Palace.
* Skansen: excellent open-air museum.

Opposite: *Two guards outside the Royal Palace, Gamla Stan.*

Above: *Öhrström's obelisk in Sergels Torg is lit up at night.*

THE STOCKHOLM BLOODBATH

The executions of 80 or so members of the Swedish elite in 1520 took place in Stortorget, still Gamla Stan's main square, but then standing beside Tre Kronor, the original Stockholm palace. It rained heavily that day and bloody water rushed down the steep streets leading away from the square in what must have been an appalling sight for the city folk.

tected by using large wooden beams across the adjacent water channels. 'Stockholm' means 'tree-trunk island'. Sturluson calls his pile-formed island *Stocksiendet* and traces of 11th-century piles have actually been found during excavations. But Stockholm could equally well refer to Birger Jarl's wooden beams.

Birger Jarl's new town was on what is now **Stadsholmen** and soon had a splendid castle, a church, a monastery and a nunnery. When Birger Jarl's successor, King Magnus Ladulås, died in 1290 he was buried in the church – St Nicolai Kyrka – an indication of the growing importance of the town. Just 30 years later **Köpmangatan**, at the heart of Stadsholmen (Gamla Stan), is mentioned by name, the oldest named street in the city. In 1391 the Danish Queen Margrethe besieged the city, leading to the creation of the Kalmar Union in 1397. Though the Swedish arm of the Union was administered from Stockholm's castle, the city was not yet the declared capital of the country.

In 1471 King Christian I of Denmark marched an army to Stockholm to put down an uprising headed by Sten Sture who wished to see an independent Sweden. The Danes were heavily defeated at the Battle of Brunkenberg (which took place in the area around Vasagatan and Sergels Torg), but despite this Sweden did not leave the Union. Instead, conflict between pro- and anti-Union groups rumbled on for 50 years culminating in the **Stockholm Bloodbath** of 1520. The Danish King, Christian II, agreed to meet leading Swedish merchants, nobles and clerics in the city. At a banquet in their honour Christian had them all arrested. A kangaroo court found them guilty of arson of the bishop's palace at

Sigtuna, and the next day over 80 of them – including Sten Sture's son – were beheaded in Stortorget. This finally galvanized the Swedes and a young nobleman, Gustav Eriksson, led a successful rebellion. On 6 June 1523 (National Day) he was crowned King Gustav Vasa. Despite this, it was another century before Stockholm became Sweden's official capital.

In the centuries that followed Stockholm was struck by the horrors inflicted on virtually all of Europe's major cities. Fire destroyed many of the buildings, including the original (Tre Kroner – Three Crowns) castle, and plague killed thousands. At the height of the plague it is said that up to 1000 people died daily (from a population of around 50,000). Ultimately peace and calm returned, with 18th-century Stockholm seeing a scientific and artistic renaissance. In the 19th century, industrialization brought prosperity – Stockholm's position as a leading world city was recognized by the awarding of the 1912 Olympic Games. During the last half of the 20th century the city was refurbished – a transformation that saw it increase in importance as a European commercial centre, but at the expense of the erection of some unappealing tower blocks. That, however, is a minor quibble. Spread across the islands of a glorious Baltic archipelago, Stockholm is a wonderful place and rightly on the itinerary of many looking for an interesting, exciting city.

Below: *Gamla Stan seen across the Söderström from Södermalm.*

GAMLA STAN ***

All explorations of Stockholm must start with a tour of Gamla Stan (Old Town) where the city began. At the old town's heart is the **Kungliga Slottet**, the royal palace, built to replace the Tre Kroner Castle after it burnt down in 1697 and incorporating the original castle's north wing, all that sur-

CHANGING THE ROYAL GUARD

The ceremony of the changing of the Royal Guard takes
place within the large courtyard created by the semi-
circular projecting wings at
the western end of the royal
palace. The ceremony is held
at 12:15 (13:15 Sun and
bank holidays) daily Jun–Aug
and same times Wed, Sat
and Sun Sep–May. Arrive
early for a good view.

Below: *The Royal Palace
from Skeppsholmen. The
boats are ferries which
link Stockholm's islands.*

vived (though nothing can be seen of it from the outside
as it lies behind the new façade). The new palace was
designed by Nicodemus Tessin the Younger and took 57
years to complete. It has 608 rooms and, although no
longer occupied as a residence by the royal family, is still
used for dinners and receptions. Externally the palace is
grand but not visually spectacular. At the eastern end,
two projecting wings enclose the **Logården**, a formal garden of regimented shrubs and close-cropped lawns
which can be viewed through wrought-iron gates (easier
for taller visitors).

The State Apartments are open to visitors (10:00–16:00
daily mid-May to Aug; 12:00–15:00 Tue–Sun Sep–Dec,
Feb to mid-May). The **Hall of State** is a dazzling room
which combines classical and rococo design ideas
superbly. Its centrepiece is the silver throne of Queen
Kristina, a gift to her for her coronation in 1650. It is of
forged and cast silver over a wooden frame and is the
palace's most famous treasure. Other rooms are equally
splendid and though ornate and lavishly decorated are
never outlandish or overpowering. The **Royal Chapel** is,
in style, similar to the Hall of State, but on an altogether
grander scale. It has many treasures, including pew-ends
made for the chapel of the Tre Kroner and saved from
destruction in the fire.

The palace houses several very fine museums. The **Tre Kronor Museum** occupies the surviving section of the old castle, the lower walls of which can be seen. It has models of the Tre Kronor and items rescued from it which help explore the 1000 years of royal palaces on this site (same opening times as Royal Palace). The **Palace Treasury** holds the crown jewels and regalia, while **Gustav III's Antiquities Museum** has the collection

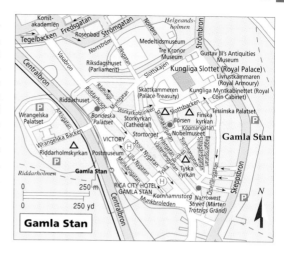

Gamla Stan

of King Gustav, and other art treasures. The **Livrust-kammaren** (Royal Armoury), which – as with the Tre Kroner Museum – can be entered separately from the palace, has some quite extraordinary items such as the stuffed and mounted horse which King Gustav II Adolf rode into battle, King Gustav III's costume from the 1792 masked ball at which he was assassinated, and the uniform King Karl XII was wearing (the boots still muddy) when he died in 1718. (Open 10:00–17:00 daily Jun–Aug; 11:00–17:00 Tue, Wed, Fri–Sun, 11:00–20:00 Thu Sep–May.)

In Slottsbacken, on the southern side of the palace, the **obelisk** was raised by King Gustav III to thank the country for its support of his Russian campaign of 1788–90. Across the wide street from the palace the **Tessinska Palatset** was built by and for Nicodemus Tessin the Younger, the palace's architect. It now houses the Governor of Stockholm. Next door, the **Kungliga Myntkabinettet**, the Royal Coin Cabinet, is one of the world's finest collections of coins and banknotes, including the world's oldest coin (625BC) and the world's largest struck coin (1644, a copper slab weighing 19.7kg/4lb), and the world's oldest banknote, from 1661. (Open 10:00–16:00 Tue–Sun.)

STOCKHOLM'S MUSEUMS

Stockholm has around 60 museums, just a few of which have been mentioned in the text. The Tourist Office publishes a leaflet listing them all, with addresses and opening times. As well as several art museums and specific history museums, there are such specialist places as a museum of wine and spirits, a toy museum, a police technology museum and one to the Nobel prize and prizewinners. Children will enjoy some of the museums, as well as Junibacken, on Djurgården close to the Vasamuseet. Based on Astrid Lindgren's *Pippi Longstocking* stories, this is not a museum, there being plenty of opportunity for interactive play as well as a mini-train through scenes from the books.

Above: *Stortorget is one of the old town's most picturesque spots.*

At the western end of Slottsbacken, beyond the obelisk, the **Storkyrkan** is Stockholm's cathedral. Built on the site of Birger Jarl's first town church it dates from 1306 (though with later additions) and is the city's oldest building. The clock and bell tower – 66m (216ft) high – was added in 1743. Inside there are royal pews from the 17th century, a superb silver altar and a life-size statue of St George and the Dragon. This latter, one of the artistic masterpieces of northern Europe, was carved of oak and elk horn by Bernt Notke of Lübeck in 1489.

Beside the cathedral is **Stortorget**, scene of the Stockholm Bloodbath. From it narrow alleys lead downhill: they are a joy to wander. Follow **Västerlånggatan**, the main street of Gamla Stan, and be sure to find **Mårten Trotzigs Gränd** which, at just 1m, is the old town's narrowest street.

On the western side of Stadsholmen stands the Baroque **Riddarhuset**, one of the city's most beautiful buildings. It was the original parliament house. Beside it, the **Bondeska Palatset** is now the Swedish Supreme Court. Over the bridge beside the Riddarhuset is **Riddarholmen**, an island on which stands **Riddarholmskyrkan**, the church which is the burial place of Swedish royalty. The church stands on the site of a 13th-century monastery and all but two of Sweden's monarchs since Gustav II Adolf rest here. In the square beside it is a **statue of Birger Jarl**, founder of the city.

CENTRAL STOCKHOLM **

From the northern side of the royal palace, bridges cross the water to **Helgeandsholmen**. Here stand the **Riksdagshuset**, the parliament building, and the **Riksbank**, the state bank, built in 1905–06. The two, now combined, are the seat of the Swedish parliament. Tours of the building are organized daily in summer (an English guide is available).

In the small park on Helgeandsholmen is the entrance to the **Medeltidsmuseum**, an underground museum built into the remains of medieval Stockholm's defences. The museum includes an exceptional 16th-century ship, a reconstructed medieval square complete with pillory and gallows, and a refurbished medieval harbour. Open 11:00–18:00 Tue–Thu, 11:00–16:00 Fri–Mon, Jul–Aug; 11:00–16:00 Tue and Thu–Sun, 11:00–18:00 Wed, Sep–Jun.

From the **Norrbro** (the bridge that crosses from Helgeandsholmen to Gustav Adolfs Torg) there is, looking towards the left, a marvellous view of the waterside buildings of the city. At the far end is **Rosenbad**, built in the 19th century and housing the offices of the prime minister and cabinet ministers. Two buildings along from the Rosenbad is the **Sagerska Palatset**, the prime minister's official residence. Finally, before Gustav Adolfs Torg, is the **Arvfurstens Palats**, built in the late 18th century for King Gustav III's sister. It is now the home of the Swedish Foreign Office. **Gustav Adolfs Torg** is dominated by an equestrian statue of Gustav II Adolf.

Just behind him is the **Dansmuseet** (Museum of Dance), open 11:00–16:00 Mon–Sat Jun–Aug; 11:00–16:00 Tue–Fri, 12:00–16:00 Sat, Sun Sep–May), while in the top left corner the **Medelhavsmuseet** has collections of Egyptian, Greek and Roman antiquities (open 11:00–20:00 Tue, 11:00–16:00 Wed–Fri, and 12:00–17:00 Sat, Sun). To the right is the 18th-century **Opera House** which has a wonderful interior: if you cannot take in a performance,

---

ROSENBAD

The curious name derives from a bathhouse that occupied the site in the 17th century and was famous for its choice of camomile, lily or rose water, the last being, in Swedish, a *rosenbad*.

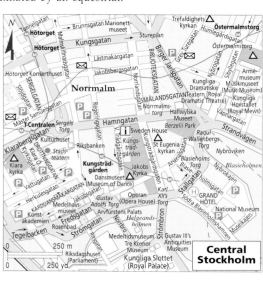

Central Stockholm

SERGELS TORG

The striking obelisk in Sergels Torg is the work of Edvin Öhrström who named it *Crystal Vertical Accent in Glass and Steel*, which is instructive if not entirely illuminating. On the topic of illumination, the obelisk looks splendid at night when lit by the double circle of pavement lights.

be sure to see the fabulous 28m (31yd) gold foyer. Behind the Opera House is **Jacobs Kyrka**, completed in very elegant style in the 1640s.

Beside the Opera House is a **statue of King Karl XII** by JB Molin who was also responsible for the **fountain** in the formal garden. The open space beyond – Kungsträdgården, the King's kitchen garden, as that is what it once was – is a favourite with city dwellers in the summer. Turn left onto Hamngatan passing, to the right, the NK clock above the store. Ahead is **Sergels Torg**, a two-level square where, in summer, there are often street theatre acts or temporary exhibitions.

North of Sergels Torg the **Hötorget Konserthuset** is a marvellous building decorated with a superb sculpture, *Orpheus*, by Carl Miller. On a more sombre note a nearby plaque marks the spot where Olof Palme was gunned down in 1986.

Eastwards along Hamngatan from Kungsträdgården the visitor reaches the **Hallwylska Museet**, a private palace with an impressive façade behind which is a lavish interior that is now a museum of the eclectic collections of former owners. (Guided tours only, in English at certain times: check Tourist Office for details.) Beyond is the magnificent white marble **Royal Dramatic Theatre**, behind which is the city's **Music**

Right: *The Opera House, left, and Jacobs Kyrka from Kungsträdgården.*

Museum (open 11:00–16:00 Tue–Sun) and the **Kungliga Hovstallet**, the Royal Mews. The Hovstallet is open to visitors who can admire the state carriages and the horses that still draw them on special occasions. (Guided tours only, in English at certain times: check Tourist Office for details.)

Blasieholmen ✶

To the south of the Hallwylska Palatset is Blasieholmen, a finger of land poked out towards the island of Skeppsholmen, the walk taking the visitor through **Raoul Wallenbergs Torg** (*see*

Blasieholmen and Skeppsholmen

panel page 19). To the south, **Blasieholms Torg** is flanked by impressive buildings including two very old palaces, at No. 6 and No. 8, attended by a pair of proud bronze horses. Exit the square along Stallgatan and turn left at the very grand **Grand Hôtel** in which the year's Nobel prizewinners are accommodated.

Walk past the Grand Hôtel to reach the **National Museum**. Built in the 1860s, the museum has Sweden's largest collection of art – painting, sculpture and decorative art. Pride of place goes to Rembrandt's *Conspiracy of the Batavians*, Alexander Roslin's *The Lady with the Veil* which has become an icon of the 18th-century Swedish renaissance, and Johan Tobias Sergel's *The Faun*, another fine 18th-century work. As well as the art works, the museum also has a good collection of furniture, porcelain, silver and glass. Open 11:00–20:00 Tue, Thu, 11:00–17:00 Wed, Fri–Sun.

Above: *Some of the exhibits which stand outside the Moderna Museet (Modern Art Museum) on Skeppsholmen.*

Skeppsholmen **

From the end of Blasieholmen, beyond the museum, a wrought-iron bridge crosses to **Skeppsholmen** which, in the 17th century, was a base for the Swedish navy. Today many of the old naval buildings have been transformed into museums and exhibition/concert areas making the island one of the most exciting places in the city. The prominent building as the island is reached is Skeppsholmen Church, built in the 1820s. Behind it is the **Östasiastiskamuseet** (Far Eastern Antiquities Museum), which has a quite stunning array of history and art works including what is claimed to be the finest Chinese art collection outside of China. As well as the Chinese art, and an important archaeological collection from China, the museum covers Korea and Japan, and also has pieces from India. Open 12:00–17:00 Tue–Sun (until 20:00 on Tue).

Beside the museum is another – the **Moderna Museet**. This museum is housed in a part-new building designed by the Catalan architect Rafael Moneo (who won a competition against 210 other entries in 1989; the museum opened in 1998). The striking building displays a collection of contemporary art, including paintings, sculpture, photographs and videos, by both Swedish and international artists. (Open 11:00–20:00 Tue–Thu, 11:00–18:00 Fri–Sun.)

Next to the modern art museum, and sharing an entrance and restaurant with it, is the **Arkitekturmuseet** which explores 2000 years of Scandinavian and World architecture. Open 11:00–18:00 Tue–Sun (20:00 on Tue).

Behind the two museums is a **festival area** originally created for the Millennium celebrations and now a major outdoor venue (for instance, for the excellent Jazz and Blues festival held annually in late July). Next to the area is a **wooden crane** dating from 1751 when it worked in the naval dockyard.

THE AF CHAPMAN

The ship is a three-masted full-rigger built in 1888 at Whitehaven in England. After a career as a freighter, the ship was sailed to Sweden in 1915. Renamed for a famous Gothenburg shipbuilder, Frederik Henrik af Chapman, the ship was used as a training vessel. Since 1949 she has been berthed at Skeppsholmen where she is now one of the world's most romantic youth hostels. Visitors who are not staying at the hostel can board to admire the ship.

On the opposite side of the island, to the right as you reach it, is the *af Chapman* (*see* panel, page 40). From it, continue along Västra Brobänken. There is another hostel to the left, then the **Crafts and Design Society** building and the **Royal College of Fine Arts** (identified by the cast-iron version of the Florentine boar) are passed before the bridge to Kastellholmen is reached.

Djurgården ★★★

From Raoul Wallenbergs Torg (*see* page 39) the visitor can follow **Strandvägen**. To the left is a row of elegant houses built by Stockholm's wealthiest in the 1900s, while to the right is a row of historic sailing ships. When a bridge (Djurgårdsbron), to the right, is reached, go left for a quick detour to the **Historiska Museet** in Narvavägen. This superb museum has an amazing collection exploring Sweden's early history. The Bäckaskog woman, a skeleton excavated from a burial pit, is thought to be 10,000 years old. The Viking collection is outstanding, particularly the jewellery, but the real treasure is in the underground **Gold Room** with its items from the Bronze Age to the Middle Ages. The Elizabeth reliquary, made in the 11th century as a drinking goblet, but altered in the early 13th century to act as a depository for the skull of St Elizabeth, is phenomenal. (Open 11:00–17:00 Tue–Sun.)

A right turn over the Djurgårdsbron takes the visitor on to **Djurgården**, once a royal hunting ground with herds of reindeer and elk, then a park for city

Below: *The striking Nordiskamuseet which has a marvellous collection exploring everyday life in Sweden from medieval times.*

dwellers, and now both a park and site of several of Stockholm's most important museums.

The first building on the island houses, behind its impressive façade, the **Nordiskamuseet**. The Nordiska explores Sweden's cultural history from the Middle Ages to the present. The collection includes a series of table settings which are still such a feature of Scandinavian design, and paintings by the author August Strindberg. (Open 10:00–17:00 daily; closed Mon Sep to mid-Jun.)

Beyond the Nordiska, in a building whose roof rather gives the game away about what is held inside, is the **Vasamuseet**, surely one of the most remarkable museums not only in Sweden, but in the world, and for many the highlight of a visit to Stockholm. In 1625 King Gustaf II Adolf had 1000 oaks felled for the building of a huge and richly decorated ship that was to be the pride of the Swedish navy. On 10 August 1628 the *Vasa*, as the ship was called, sailed on her maiden voyage. That voyage lasted just 1300m (1420yd). A light breeze pushed the ship over, she righted herself for an instant, then keeled over. Water rushed into the gun ports and the ship sank in minutes. Fifty of the 100 or so officers and men (and assorted wives and children) on board drowned. An attempt to raise the ship failed, but 30 years later a diving bell was used to raise most of the 64 guns.

In 1953 Anders Franzén became interested in the *Vasa*. By examining documents he worked out where she lay, in 32m (100ft) of water off Beckholmen Island. A salvage operation then began which resulted in the ship being raised in 1961 (on 24 April, Vega Day). After years of preservation work on the timber the ship was moved to the new museum building in 1988. Although the state of preservation of the *Vasa* is now well known, nothing can prepare visitors for their first sight of the ship. Lighting in the museum is dim to prevent damage to the timber,

so visiting eyes must adjust – and out of the twilight looms a virtually complete, authentic 17th-century warship. The statues and carvings are astonishingly well preserved. Originally many would have been painted so that the ship would have seemed almost miraculous to the ordinary city dweller. Open 09:30–19:00 daily mid-June to mid-Aug;

10:00–17:00 (until 20:00 on Wed) mid-Aug to mid-June.

Above: *The* Vasa, *centrepiece of one of the most remarkable museums in Europe.*

Close to the Vasamuseet, the **Museifartygen** (Ships Museum) consists of the early 20th-century ice-breaker *Sankt Erik* and the lightship *Finngrundet*. Open 12:00–17:00 daily Jun–Aug (until 19:00 in July). Beyond the Vasamuseet is a memorial to the 852 people who died when the ferry *Estonia* sank during the night of 27–28 September 1994 on its voyage to Stockholm from the Estonian capital Tallinn. The memorial is a quiet place and a moving tribute to the dead.

On again is the **Biologiskamuseet**, the first museum of its type in the world when it opened in 1893. It depicts almost all Scandinavia's bird and mammal species, mostly in dioramas of their natural habitats. (Open 10:00–16:00 daily Apr–Sep; 10:00–15:00 Tue–Sun Oct–Mar.)

Further on are the **Tivoli** amusement park, Stockholm's answer to the Copenhagen original, and **Skansen**, the world's oldest open-air museum (founded in 1891) which depicts 500 years of Swedish history through some 150 buildings which have been brought from all over Sweden and re-erected on the site. The site has been planted with flora from across the country. There is also a small zoo of Scandinavian mammals (and also a children's zoo). The site is home to numerous festivals and concerts throughout the year. There are excellent craft workshops, shops, a restaurant and café. Altogether Skansen is an absolute delight. Houses: open 11:00–17:00 daily May–Sep; Park: open 10:00–16:00 daily, (closes at 20:00 in May, 22:00 Jun–Aug and 17:00 Sep).

LIFE AND DEATH ON BOARD

As well as the ship, hundreds of artefacts were recovered during the *Vasa* salvage operation. These have been beautifully arranged to give a compelling glimpse of the grim, harsh life of the ordinary seaman on board a vessel such as *Vasa*. There are also displays which show the horrors of medieval naval warfare. Cannon fire produces horrific injuries, but somehow the idea of such mutilation seems far worse, not only in an era of relatively limited medical care but in the hot, smoky hell of a claustrophobically small warship.

OUTER STOCKHOLM

Although Stockholm's major sites lie close to the centre, the outer areas of the town hold much of interest. **Östermalm**, north of Strandvägen, is the site of several fine collections. To the east is **Ladugårds-gärdet**, once a royal farm, then a military training ground before being reclaimed as a city space.

Above: Sången *(The Song), one of the statues at the Stadshuset.*
Opposite: *The Chinese Pavilion at Drottningholm.*

Bordering the sea there are several museums, particularly the city's excellent maritime museum. Close by is the 155m (508ft) **Kaknäs Tower**, a telecommunications centre with a fine restaurant and viewing platforms for an unrivalled view of the city.

West of the city centre, **Kungsholmen** is the site of Stockholm's city hall and law courts, originally conceived as one building, but built as two. The **Rådhuset**, housing the law courts, was completed in 1915, eight years before the completion of the more elaborate city hall. North of Kungsholmen lies **Vasastaden**, an area of fine parks and good restaurants. North again is **Ekoparken**, the world's first national city park. Here, within just a few kilometres of the city centre, herons breed and other wildlife thrives. One particularly fine area is **Hagaparken** with its array of curious buildings erected by King Gustav III as part of his plan to create a Swedish version of Versailles. That great plan died with the king, but what was built is a delight, particularly the extraordinary **Koppartälten** (Copper Tent), erected as stables and now a restaurant.

Finally, head south of Gamla Stan to **Södermalm**, birthplace of Greta Garbo. **Fjällgatan**, to the east of Slussen, is often claimed to be Stockholm's most beautiful street. In nearby **Stigbergsgatan** the picturesque Söder cottages are the best preserved of Stockholm's 18th-century wooden buildings.

STOCKHOLM'S STADSHUSET

Designed by Ragner Östberg and completed in 1923, the Stadshuset (City Hall) on Kungsholmen is now a symbol of the city as well as a functioning city hall. The main tower is topped by the Tre Kronor, the symbol of Sweden. Inside, the Golden Room has mosaics created from over 19 million sections of gold leaf, while the Blue Hall is the scene of the annual presentation of the awards to the winners of the Nobel prizes.

AROUND THE ARCHIPELAGO
Drottningholm **

Of the sites a little further out from the centre of Stockholm pride of place must go to **Drottningholm**. The site is named for the *drottning* (queen) of King Johann III, but the castle built for her was destroyed by fire in 1661. The following year Nicodemus Tessin the Elder began work on a replacement. After his death the work was continued by his son, Nicodemus the Younger, and by later architects. What they created, which has been the private home of the royal family since 1981, is the finest Swedish palace and one of the best in Europe.

The palace interior is opulent, as might be imagined, yet never overly ostentatious. **Queen Hedvig Eleonora's Bedroom** is the most lavish: it took 15 years to complete and is, not surprisingly, Sweden's most expensive Baroque interior. Much more understated and intimate are the beautiful **Green Drawing Room** and the elegant **Queen Lovisa Ulrika's Library**. Many of the rooms have priceless paintings, the most effective being the superb trompe l'oeil by Johan Sylvius on the staircase.

Next to the palace is the **Slottsteater**, the oldest theatre in the world preserved in its original state. The theatre was built in 1766 and the original stage machinery still operates during the regular summer performances. The theatre has a museum of its history. Behind the two buildings lies the palace's Baroque garden which began in the 1670s with the aim of creating perfect symmetry. Interest in the garden, however, declined after King Gustav III's reign and by the 19th century much had been demolished. Only in the 1950s was interest rekindled. The aim was to recreate Paradise (the name given to the original) as far

THE PALACE THEATRE

After the death of King Gustav III in 1792 the theatre fell into disuse. In the 1920s it was rediscovered and far from having decayed was in excellent condition. It was refurbished, the original candle lighting being replaced with electricity and the stage machinery being renovated. The machinery included wind and thunder machines, wind noise being generated by a canvas-covered cylinder, thunder by turning a wooden box loaded with stones. The theatre museum includes 17th- and 18th-century scenery paintings and original costumes.

Opposite: *The sea journey to Vaxholm Castle is as worthwhile as the castle itself.*
Below: The Hand of God, *one of the most famous sculptures in the Milles Gården.*

as possible. Work is still ongoing, but the ideas of the original, with its topiary and fountains, are being faithfully followed. North of the formal Paradise Garden King Gustav III created another. Though English (naturalistic) in style, the formality of Paradise was not completely abandoned, with avenues of trees off-setting the pure landscape of the lakes and islands.

South of the Paradise Garden is another section of landscaped park in which stands the **Chinese Pavilion** – not the original which so delighted Queen Lovisa Ulrika, but a replacement built 10 years later when the first one had rotted away. The new pavilion is decorated in oriental style and has a wealth of Chinese and Japanese art work. Close by, the **Guard's Tent** is not quite what it seems. Though tent-like in appearance it is actually painted iron sheeting. It houses a museum of the palace and park. (All buildings open: 11:00–16:30 daily Jun–Aug; 12:00–16:30 daily May; 13:00–15:30 daily Sep.)

Birka *

West of Drottningholm, **Birka** is the site of the 8th-century 'capital' of the Svea kingdom centred on Mälaren, the first real Swedish town. The town was abandoned in the 10th century in favour of Sigtuna, and the island of Björkö, on which Birka stands, gradually returned to nature. Today Björkö is popular for its natural beauty and the museum which explores its ancient past. Museum open: 11:00–17:00 daily May–Sep (until 18:00 Jul to mid-Aug).

Sigtuna *

Sigtuna, now Sweden's oldest town, lies north of Stockholm. Its main street, Storagatan, is probably the oldest in the country (though the original main street lies below the

current one, beneath 3m/10ft of the accumulated debris of history). Sigtuna also boasts several fine old churches such as the brick-built Mariakyrkan which was part of a 13th-century monastery; Scandinavia's smallest town hall which was built in 1744; and an excellent museum which explores the town's Viking and early medieval heritage. Open 12:00–16:00 daily; closed Mon, Sep–May.

Close to the town are two fine castles: **Rosersbergs Slott**, built in the 1630s and with beautiful gardens (open 11:00–15:00 daily May–Aug; 11:00–15:00 Sat, Sun, Sep), and **Steninge Slott**, built in 1705 by Tessin the Younger. Steninge is now a cultural centre, with art and crafts workshops and a excellent restaurant (open 11:00–16:00 Sun–Fri mid-Jun to mid-Aug, 11:00–14:00 Sat; 11:00–14:00 Sat, Sun mid-Aug to mid-Nov, Jan to mid-Jun).

Vaxholm **

Finally, northeast of Stockholm, beyond Milles Gården, is **Vaxholm**, best reached by a boat ride from the city which, travelling through the archipelago, is a joy in itself. The east end of the island is dominated by an off-shore fortress, built in the 19th century. After it lost its strategic importance the fortress became a prison: it now houses an excellent military museum (open 11:45–15:45 daily Jun–Aug). On the main island, the waterfront area is delightful, particularly the wooden houses of Hamngatan and Söderhamn.

Stockholm at a Glance

BEST TIMES TO VISIT

Most people visit in summer – with the city's best sites being within walking distance of each other, warm days are a real bonus for exploration. Djurgården and Skansen are colourful in spring and autumn, and even in winter when the new snow is on the ground. Stockholm winters, however, can be very cold.

GETTING THERE

By air: Most visitors arrive by air, landing at **Arlanda** airport about 40km (25 miles) north of the city centre. From Arlanda a bus service (the *Flygbussarna*) runs to and from Central Station. That journey takes twice as long (about 45 minutes), but costs half as much as the train to Central Station. Stockholm also has two other airports. **Bromma** lies quite close to the city centre, but is chiefly used for domestic flights. Some international carriers use it by flying into Malmö and then taking an internal flight. The third airport, **Skavsta**, is becoming increasingly popular with European budget airlines. Bromma and Skavsta have bus services into the city.
By train: The Öresund link between Copenhagen and Malmö connects Sweden by train to the European rail service. Sweden can therefore easily be reached by train (though changes of trains may be necessary). These

trains arrive at Central Station.
By road: The Öresund link also makes it possible to drive to Stockholm without taking a ferry. Drivers should be aware that the **E22** (marked in green on Swedish maps) which links Malmö with Stockholm is neither a motorway nor a dual carriageway. For most of its 640km (400 miles) the E22 is ordinary road – passing through beautiful country, but not the high-speed link many assume. It takes a day to make the journey, whereas the trip from Gothenburg to Stockholm is indeed on a motorway and takes about 4 hours.
By ferry: Stockholm is linked to Helsinki and Tallinn by ferry.

GETTING AROUND

Stockholm has a very efficient **metro** system, the Tunnelbana. The three lines (though all three have branch lines) meet at Central Station. The pricing is by zone, but most of the city sights lie in the central zone. The Stockholm Card offers free travel on the Tunnelbana and the city bus service (and free admission to around 70 museums and sites). The **bus** system is also very good, utilizing a system where blue 'feeder' (outer-city) buses transport passengers into the city where red buses take over for inner-city journeys. As most sites are within walking distance, most visitors use the metro and buses spar-

ingly. A worthwhile trip is the No. 7 **tram** through Djurgården to Skansen. It is, however, not covered by the Stockholm Card. Stockholm lost its trams in 1967, but here, as elsewhere, the benefits of trams have been noticed.

WHERE TO STAY

A range of accommodation is available in Stockholm. The main Tourist Information Office offers assistance.

LUXURY

Victory Hotel, Lilla Nygatan 5, 111 28 Stockholm, tel: 8 5064 0000, fax: 8 5064 0010. Marvellous early 17th-century building on the western side of Gamla Stan with a Lord Nelson theme. Small, pricey rooms, but very tasteful. Has one of the city's finest restaurants.
Radisson SAS Royal Viking Hotel, Vasagatan 1, 101 24 Stockholm, tel: 8 5065 4000, fax: 8 5065 4001. A modern skyscraper close to Central Station. All conceivable facilities; excellent fish restaurant.
Grand Hôtel Stockholm, Södra Blaisieholmshamnen 8, 103 27 Stockholm, tel: 8 679 3500, fax: 8 611 8686. Very grand, outside and inside. The mix of the old-fashioned with the more modern refurbishment works really well.

MID-RANGE

Rica City Hotel Gamla Stan, Lilla Nygatan 25, 111 28

Stockholm at a Glance

Stockholm, tel: 8 723 7250, fax: 8 723 7259. In the same street as the Victory. Fine 17th-century building recently, and well, refurbished. Perhaps not as grand as its near neighbour, but very pleasant.

Queen's Hotel, Drottning-gatan 71A, 111 36 Stockholm, tel: 8 249 260, fax: 8 217 620. Charming, with marble staircases, an old-fashioned lift and an old-fashioned attitude towards service. Part of shopping area close to Sergels Torg.

Stureparkens Gästvåning, Sturegatan 58, 114 36 Stockholm, tel: 8 662 7230, fax: 8 661 5713. In Öster-malm, north of Hallwylska Museet. Small hotel on the fourth floor of a six-storey building. Cheerful, pleasant, and close to sights.

BUDGET

Gustaf af Klint, Stadsgård-skajen 153, 116 45 Stockholm, tel: 8 640 4077/78, fax: 8 640 6416. A boat hostel. Superb location on the Södermalm waterfront. Use the ferry to reach Skepps-holmen and Djurgården.

Good Night Hotell Danielsson, Västmanna-gatan 5, 111 24 Stockholm, tel: 8 411 1065/411 1076, fax: 8 411 1036/31 7020. Cheap and pleasant. In Vasastaden so a ride to the centre is necessary. There are local bus stops, while the

Odenplan metro station is 10-minute walk away.

WHERE TO EAT

Stockholm has a terrific range of restaurants. Two superb, but expensive, restaurants have already been mentioned:

LUXURY

Leijontornet, Lilla Nygatan 5, tel: 8 14 2355. Housed in a medieval cellar; very stylish. Extensive menu includes meat, fish and vegetarian. **Stockholm Fiske**, in the Radisson SAS Royal Viking Hotel. Phenomenal, but expensive, fish restaurant.

MID-RANGE – BUDGET

Bakfickan, Operahuset, King Karl XII Torg, tel: 8 676 5809. Art Nouveau décor; superb cooking and service. **Grand National**, Regerings-gatan 74, tel: 8 24 8052. Great Swedish cooking eaten with a background of quiet jazz.

SHOPPING

The area around Sergels Torg offers the best shopping in the city. All the international names are here as well as some of the better Scandinavian design companies. The best departmental store is **Nordiska Kompaniet** (NK) in Hamngatan. **DesignTorget** in the Kulturhuset, Sergels Torg 3, is a showcase for new work and a good place for souvenirs.

TOURS AND EXCURSIONS

The Tourist Information Office has details of the numerous tours. *Stiftelsen Skärgårds-båten*, the Stockholm steam-ships, are a great way of touring the archipelago. The Stockholm Sightseeing boats are good and offer dinner cruises. The modern ships of Strömma Kanalbolaget offer meals on longer cruises. Try a cruise in the Svea Viking, a Viking longboat which sails daily (Jun–Aug) from the Royal Palace to explore the archipelago. During the trip Viking-inspired food is served; rowing is not compulsory (or even necessary).

USEFUL CONTACTS

Tourist Information Office, Kulturehuset, Sergels Torg 1, tel: 8 789 2490. This has more leaflets than could be safely carried and visitors can buy a Stockholm Card, book hotel rooms, theatre tickets, etc. **Hotellcentralen**, Central Station, tel: 8 789 2490, fax: 8 791 8666. Primarily a hotel booking service but also has general tourist information and sells Stockholm Cards. **Swedish Travel and Tourism Council**, Box 3030, 103 61 Stockholm, tel: 8 725 5500, fax: 8 725 5531. Has general information on Sweden. **P6**, Stockholm International, broadcasts English language programmes (and other languages, chiefly German) on 89.6MHz.

3
Central Sweden

Many centuries ago, a navigable river linked the freshwater lake of Mälaren to the Baltic, offering a place of safety from which the ships of the early Vikings traded with the towns of what are now the other Baltic states. The security of Mälaren allowed a powerful kingdom to develop as the Svea tribe expanded their influence. This kingdom, *Svea Rike*, became Sverige, the birthplace of modern Sweden.

As might be expected of the root of the country, the land west of Stockholm is studded with sites important to Sweden's history. **Uppsala**, **Eskilstuna** and **Västerås** all have outstanding historical sites, the **Gamla Uppsala** site being of particular significance. Uppsala, Sweden's fourth largest city, is also famous for its university and its association with **Carolus Linnaeus**, the man who brought order to the classification of plants and animals. Centuries after forming the foundation from which Sweden grew, the area led the industrialization of the country, the iron, copper and silver mines providing the cash and raw materials that were the basis of the heavy engineering for which the area is still famous. The ruins of these mines at **Ängelsberg**, **Sala** and **Kopparberg** are among the most important industrial archaeological sites in Europe.

Today **Svea** is the name given to the six regions which lie across central Sweden. In this chapter we explore most of these, leaving Dalarna, where rugged northern Sweden begins in earnest, until later. The big towns of the region have already been mentioned, but there are others of interest such as **Nyköping** in Sörmland, with its beautiful

Don't Miss

*** Gamla Uppsala: birthplace of Sweden.
*** Örebro Castle: one of the most picturesque castles in Sweden.
** Gyllenhjelmsgatan: beautiful street of old wooden houses in Strängnäs.
** Sigurdsristningen: remarkable Viking rock carving.
* Ängelsberg: interesting industrial archaeology site.

Opposite: *Uppsala Cathedral, where Gustav Vasa and Carolus Linnaeus are buried and Swedish monarchs crowned.*

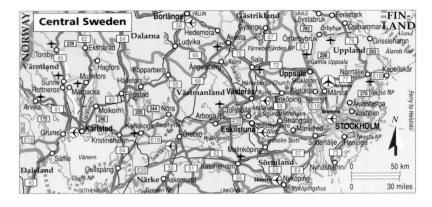

river and castle, and **Örebro** with what many consider the most beautiful of Swedish castles. To the west of Örbro the country becomes more rugged as the Norwegian border is approached. **Karlstad**, a port on the Vänern, is the centre for exploring this wild, but rewarding area.

UPPLAND
Gamla Uppsala ★★★

About 1500 years ago the religious centre of the Svea was at **Gamla Uppsala** (Old Uppsala), a site about 4km (2.5 miles) north of the present city centre. There stand three grave mounds in which, legend has it, lie the bodies of Adil, Aun and Egils, three kings of the pre-Viking era. A sacred grove of trees grew here and pagan rites were carried out involving the sacrifice of people and animals. It is claimed that in one festival, held every nine years, nine victims would be hung from the trees, their bodies allowed to rot. It is probable that when the Viking pantheon of gods became established they, too, were worshipped at Gamla Uppsala. When Christianity replaced paganism a church was built on the site of the sacrifices. Enlarged in the 15th century, it was the scene of the coronation of Swedish kings until the new cathedral was built. A museum explores the history of the site (open 11:00–17:00 daily May–Aug; 12:00–15:00 Sun Sep–Apr). The church, partially ruined after a devastating fire, can also be visited.

Uppsala **

The **city of Uppsala** grew up away from the pagan site. The **cathedral**, the largest in Scandinavia, took 175 years to build, being consecrated only in 1435. It is a huge brick building with elegant spires and a beautiful semi-circular apse, and houses the tombs of many famous Swedes including King Gustav Vasa and Linnaeus. The cathedral treasury includes priceless objects such as Gustav Vasa's sword. The king was responsible for the construction of the **castle**, south of the cathedral (open 12:00–16:00 Wed–Fri, 11:00–17:00 Sat, Sun). The castle was partially destroyed by fire in 1702. In the south wing of what remains is the **Konstmuseet** (Art Museum) with a collection of Swedish and international contemporary art. The ruins also hold the **Vasa Vignettes**, waxworks which illustrate the (often bloody) history of the castle.

Uppsala has more than a dozen museums – some of them, such as the tractor museum (which is dedicated to the provision of gas and electricity and disposal of sewage within the city) and several others on the university and its faculties, will be of interest chiefly to specialists. Of more general interest is the **Uppland Museum**, exploring the history of the region (open 12:00–17:00 Tue–Sun). Art lovers will enjoy **Bror Hjorth's House** with its collection of work by the naïve modernist. Open 12:00–16:00 Tue–Sun (Thu, Sat, Sun only Oct–Apr). Many visitors will want to see the *Codex Argentius*, the 6th-century Bible in the old Scandinavian language in the **Carolina Rediviva Library**. Open 09:00–20:00 Mon–Fri (until 17:00 mid-Jun to mid-Aug), 11:00–16:00 Sat. There are also several sites dedicated to **Carolus Linnaeus** – a museum with a collection of memorabilia, his two houses, which include much on his life and work, the Linnaeus Garden with many species planted by him, and the Botanical Gardens which include shrubs that he brought to the city.

CARL VON LINNÉ

Carl von Linné (Carolus Linnaeus) was born in Råshult in 1707 but is famous for his association with Uppsala University which he joined in 1728 after studying at Lund. He was a botanist whose travels in Sweden were important for cataloguing its flora. His most important innovation was the creation of a hierarchical, systematic naming system which allowed order to be brought to the formerly haphazard way of classifying plants. This system, now extended to animals, is the basis of the present method of classifying the natural world.

Below: *The burial mounds of Sweden's pre-Viking kings at Gamla Uppsala.*

Beyond Uppsala

South of Uppsala are two fine castles. **Wik Slott** is one of Sweden's best-preserved medieval castles, beautifully sited on a bay of Mälaren (guided tours in summer: ask at the Tourist Office for details). **Skokloster** dates back to the 17th-century and houses a phenomenal collection of over 50,000 items – weapons, tools, furniture, silverware, etc. (guided tours all year: ask at the Tourist Office for details).

East of Uppsala is **Norrtälje**, a delightful little town with old buildings set beside the river. The town's **Roslagen Museum** explores the history of the local area and has a good collection on local shipping (open 11:00–16:00 Mon–Fri; also 11:00–14:00 Sat mid-May to mid-Aug).

To the north there are fine coastal towns including picturesque **Grisslehamn**, from where boats cross to Åland, the Finnish tax-free haven, and **Östhammar** with its wooden buildings. To the northwest, **Forsmark** was once a local centre for iron smelting. This industrial history seems at odds with the wonderful local scenery, but modernity, in the shape of a nuclear power station, soon returns. Northwest again, **Lövstabruk** is an old iron-working town with a fine late 17th-century mansion and art galleries in renovated factory buildings. South of the town the castle at **Österbybruk** was the scene of the murder of King Erik XIV. The king was taken here when his madness became apparent and was poisoned with a bowl of pea soup.

Opposite: The excellent Västerås Art Museum is housed in the old town hall.
Below: An old house in Norrtälje, once a regional capital, but now a quieter old town.

Heading west from Österbybruk, the visitor passes through wonderful country before turning south towards Uppsala. By continuing west, this return can be made through **Härkeberga**, where the 14th-century church has a fine wooden tower, and **Kaplensgård** is a well-preserved 18th-century farm.

Västmanland
Västerås *

Southwest of Uppsala lies **Västerås**, Sweden's sixth largest city. Nearby are a number of prehistoric burial mounds including Anundshög, the largest in Sweden, as well as several stone settings. The actual site of the city, tucked into a bay of Mälaren, does not, however, appear to have such a long history. Today even the old buildings that do exist, close to the Svartån River, are dominated by modern shopping malls, the industrial buildings of Asea Brown Boveri (ABB) and other heavy engineering works. One of the old town's most interesting sites is the 14th-century

cathedral which houses the sarcophagus of the poisoned King Erik XIV. Look out, too, for the art museum, housed in the old town hall, and the local history museum.

Vallby Friluftsmuseum **

Close to Västerås the **Vallby Friluftsmuseum** (Vallby Open-air Museum) has a collection of rural timber houses brought from across Västmanland (the region around Västerås) and reconstructed on a 19th-century farmstead. There is a café, craft workshops and a shop selling site-grown vegetables. (Open 08:00–22:00 daily.)

Sala *

North of Västerås is **Sala**, a lovely little town. There are two fine old churches: the 14th-century **Sala Socken-kyrka**, which has frescoes by Albert Pictor (a well-known Swedish artist of the 15th century) and two rune stones, and **Kristinakyrka**, which was rebuilt in the 17th century when it sadly lost its 83m (270ft) spire. Elsewhere, **Väsby Kungsgård** is a 16th-century farm which now houses museums of weaponry, textiles and agricultural tools. Legend has it that King Gustav II Adolf met his favourite mistress when visiting the farm.

DEGREES CELSIUS

In 1701 Anders Celsius was born in Uppsala. A gifted mathematician, Celsius became Professor of Astronomy at Uppsala University and made several important contributions in the field. He is, however, best remembered for creating the temperature scale which now bears his name. In 1742, Celsius devised a mercury thermometer using two fixed points, the melting point of ice and the boiling point of water. Celsius chose 100 degrees and 0 degrees for these, but after his death in 1744 his colleagues reversed them to produce the more useful scale we now use.

Above: *Örebro Castle, considered by most visitors to be the finest of all Swedish castles.*
Opposite: *Brandt Contemporary Glass at Torshälla is both glass workshop and museum.*

Ängelsberg ★★

West of Sala, at **Ängelsberg**, the ironworks has recently been added to UNESCO's World Heritage list as an important early industrial site. The rare, timber-clad blast furnace dates from 1779. It and the site forge have been maintained in near-perfect state (guided tours all year: ask at the Tourist Office for details). Nearby, on the shore of the Åmänningen Lake, are the remains of the world's oldest surviving oil refinery. Opened in 1875, the refinery closed in 1902, but was never dismantled.

Örebro ★★★

From Västerås the E18 heads west and then south, linking with the E20 to reach **Örebro** at the western end of Hjälmaren Lake. At the town's heart is the superb castle, one of the most photographed sites in Sweden, beautifully positioned on the Svartån River. The 13th-century castle is the office of the county governor and also the site of the town's Tourist Information Office (guided tours of the castle are organized in the summer months: ask at the Tourist Office for details).

There are several museums in the town, but by far the most interesting of these is **Wadköping**, also set beside the river, a village museum of old wooden houses now used as craft workshops. Open 11:00–17:00 Tue–Sun (closes at 16:00 Sep–Apr).

For children, **Gustavsvik**, with indoor and outdoor pools which include sand beaches, is a must (open 09:30–18:30 daily Jul; 09:30–20:30 Mon–Fri, 09:30–17:30 Sat, Sun Aug–Jun).

Kopparberg ★

North of Örebro, **Kopparberg** is named for copper mines which were active during the 17th and 18th centuries. The mine buildings are still visible, though there is little

---

THE MUSHROOM

Voted one of Sweden's architectural gems is *Svampen*, the Örebro Mushroom. This water tower in the northern part of the town is 60m (197ft) high, offers a marvellous viewpoint and has an excellent café. It is said that on a visit to Sweden Prince Faisal of Saudi Arabia was so entranced by the building that he demanded (and got) one for Riyadh.

else to convey the sense of what the place must have looked like at that time. One site that should not be missed is **Ljusnarbergskyrka**, a red-roofed church with an interior seemingly modelled on an upturned boat.

SÖRMLAND
Eskilstuna *

To the south of Mälaren lies Sörmland (or Södermanland). Its chief town is **Eskilstuna**, an early industrial town and one in which engineering is still a major employer. It also had, until recently, the unenviable record of being Sweden's most violent city, with an unusually high murder rate. Visitors will be pleased to know that this is now in the past. The Rademacher forges are a reminder of Eskilstuna's earlier iron-based prosperity. Six remain of 20 established in the 1650s. Today they are part museum, part workshop for craft ironworkers. There are also two other museums which look at the town's industrial past. In view of the town's recent history of violence the **Vapentekniskamuseet**, covering the history of firearms, seems an unfortunate choice, but is nonetheless interesting. Also fascinating is **Sörmlandsgården** to the east of the town centre. This open-air museum explores 19th-century rural life in Sörmland. Heading west from the town centre, the **Parken Zoo** has Asian lions, white tigers, and Komodo dragons among the more usual zoo animals (open 10:00–18:00 daily; closes at 16:00 May–Aug).

Torshälla *

North of Eskilstuna, **Torshälla** has a delightful centre of old wooden houses. Be sure to see *Tors Bockor* (Thor's Goat) – an extraordinary iron sculpture in the centre of the river which hints at the town's pagan origins and industrial past. The theme is continued at the **Ebelingmuseet** which has contemporary art made from steel. Works vary from the clever and intriguing to the downright odd (open 10:00–16:00 Wed–Sun).

SIGURDSRISTNINGEN

Northeast of Eskilstuna, near the 17th-century Sundbyholms Slott (which looks rather more like a row of terraced houses than a castle) is the fabulous Sigurdsristningen, a Viking rock carving that is 3m (3.3yd) long. Carved in about 1000AD it depicts part of the saga of Sigurd Fafnesbane. The hero, Sigurd, kills a huge, slender dragon watched by his horse Grani, and Regin, the headless smith. The runic inscription in the body of the dragon tells that Sigrid (a real person, not part of the myth) built the nearby bridge (of which little remains) in memory of Holmger, her husband.

THE NYKÖPING BANQUET

In the late 13th century, King Magnus Ladulås built a castle at Nyköping. Magnus had three sons and in 1317 one of these, Birger, invited the other two, Erik and Valdemar, to a banquet at the castle. The three men ate a splendid banquet before retiring to bed. As Erik and Valdemar slept, Birger's men grabbed them and threw them into the castle dungeon. Birger locked the door and hurled the key into the river leaving his two brothers to starve to death. Each year the banquet, but not its awful aftermath, is re-enacted in the town. A rusty key, which was fished out of the river in the 19th century and is said to be the actual one Birger threw, is now on display.

Strängnäs **

East of Eskilstuna is **Strängnäs**. Gyllenhjelmsgatan, a street of wooden houses in the town, has frequently been claimed to be the most beautiful street in Sweden. The city's cathedral is also worth visiting to see the monument to King Karl IX which is topped by a mounted rider in gilded copper armour.

Mariefred *

Mariefred, to the south, has a beautifully sited 14th-century castle – **Gripsholm Slott** – once the palace of King Gustav III. The castle now houses the Swedish National Portrait Gallery (open 10:00–16:00 daily mid-May to mid-Sep; 12:00–15:00 Sat, Sun mid-Sep to mid-May). Railway enthusiasts will also want to visit the town to ride the steam trains which run close to the inlet of Mälaren.

Malmköping *

Heading south the visitor passes through **Malmköping** where Hembrygsgården contains a collection of 17th-century wooden buildings which now house photographic, textile and coach museums. The town also has a museum of trams and another of military vehicles.

Nyköping *

Further south, **Nyköping** is a charming little place with a picturesque river and the remains of an old, and infamous, castle. It is called **Nyköpingshus** and indeed looks more like a house than a castle, though the dungeon still exists as a link with harder times. In 1665, a maid knocked a candle over and the ensuing blaze destroyed virtually the entire town and gutted the castle (open 10:00–16:00 daily).

Nyköping's 19th-century theatre is the best of its age in Sweden so it is appropriate

Below: *The monument to King Karl IX in Strängnäs Cathedral.*

that the town also has a museum (the **Gripemuseet**) of model theatres, the largest collection in Europe (open 12:00–16:00 Tue–Sun). It also has the **F-11 Museet** which explores the history of Swedish aviation. Finally, head east, towards Trosa, to visit **Nynäs Manor**, a beautiful 17th-century country house furnished to show the development of country house living over three centuries (guided tours hourly 12:00–16:00, daily Jul, Aug; Sat, Sun only May, Jun, Sep).

Above: *The floral key beside the river is a memory of the infamous Nyköping banquet.*

VÄRMLAND *

To the south of Örebro (and therefore technically not in Värmland, the westernmost of the regions of Sweden that lie west of Stockholm) is **Askersund**, a peaceful town with some very picturesque wooden houses. Southwest of the town, the **Tiveden National Park** was set up to protect one of the last remnants of southern Sweden's original forest. The forest is home to the elusive three-toed woodpecker, a black-and-white bird with a distinctive yellow cap.

North of Askersund, at **Karlskoga**, visitors can see **Björkborn Manor** where Alfred Nobel lived (from 1894) after buying the local Bofors-Gullspäng factory. His laboratory can also be visited: it stands beside the **Fiffiga Huset** where children can learn about science while having fun. It was in Karlskoga that the official 100th anniversary of the awarding of the first Nobel prizes was held, not surprisingly in view of the importance of the town to the prizes. Nobel's will was the subject of a court decision after his death. He died in San Remo, Italy, and had the court decided that was his home his living relatives would have inherited his fortune. But it decided that his legal home was Karlskoga and so his will stood.

West of Karlskoga, at **Kristinehamn**, what was once a psychiatric hospital has been converted to an art museum and a museum centred on a reconstructed

---

JOHN ERICSSON AND THE AMERICAN CIVIL WAR

John Ericsson was born in Långban, Filipstad, in 1803. After serving in the Swedish army as an engineer he went to England where he invented the screw propeller. He then went to America where he built the steam-driven, screw-propelled *Princeton* for the US navy. Unfortunately a gun on this exploded while it was being inspected by the government: President Tyler was lucky to escape death, but several officials were killed. Despite this, Ericsson built the iron-clad *Monitor* for the Union. The ship helped blockade the South during the Civil War and so helped win the Civil War. The success of the ship spelt the end of wooden warships.

Above: *Selma Lagerlöf, the Nobel prize winning author, is celebrated on Sweden's 20-kronor note.*

medieval farm and market. At nearby **Rönneberg** there is a 15m (50ft) Picasso statue. In the 1950s Picasso produced a series of sculptures and paintings, *Les dames des Mougins*. The sculptures were models for works he intended to make on a monumental scale. Although Picasso did not visit Rönneberg, he followed the construction of the work by film and photograph.

North of Kristinehamn, at **Filipstad**, there is a vast memorial to the town's most famous son, the inventor John Ericsson. A good deal more subtle is the delightful statue of Nils Ferlin, a popular Swedish poet, which sits on a bench in the town's central park. To the east, at **Hällefors**, there is an open-air gallery to the best of Swedish sculpture in Mästarnas Park, including works by Carl Milles, Bror Hjorth and Johan Tobias Sergel.

West of Karlskoga is **Karlstad**, a port of Vänern. The old quarter is picturesque and the 18th-century cathedral is worth visiting. The old town prison is now a hotel though the basement cells have been transformed into a museum. Younger visitors will enjoy the Mariebergsskogen park which mixes amusements and wildlife.

Karlstad has a statue of Selma Lagerlöf, who was born at **Mårbacka**, to the north. Ms Lagerlöf wrote books grounded in this area of Värmland. For her most famous work, *The Wonderful World of Nils*, she was awarded the Nobel Prize for Literature, and used the money to build a new house which is now a museum to her (guided tours only, May–Sep). Though little known outside Sweden, Ms Lagerlöf is famous within the country, her portrait adorning the 20-kroner note.

West of Mårbacka, at **Rottneros**, there is a beautiful park with numerous sculptures and one of the best motorcycle museums in Europe. Northwards, **Sunne**, Sweden's southernmost ski resort, is a pretty town, while **Torsby** has a car museum but is now most famous as the birthplace of Sven-Göran Eriksson, the current manager of the England football team.

WILD VÄRMLAND

At **Ekshärad**, to the east of Torsby, there is a 'beast of prey' centre which has information on the four predators which live in Värmland (and northern Sweden) but which are seen only by lucky visitors. The four are the European brown bear, the lynx, the wolf and the wolverine. The centre also looks at mankind's relationship with the four. Man, however, does not come out of this presentation with much credit.

Central Sweden at a Glance

As with nearby Stockholm, the long **summer** days are the ideal time; **winter** is best avoided unless you are intending to add a day's skiing to your itinerary.

By air: There are airports at Karlstad, Örebro and Västerås for domestic flights from Stockholm.

By train: There is a good train service which, after Karlstad, crosses Värmland to reach Norway.

By bus: The bus service is reasonable from Stockholm.

By road: Drivers will take the E18 motorway which heads north of Mälaren to reach Västerås and then continues to Örebro. From there the motorway (which has sections of 'ordinary' road) continues as a single carriageway to Karlstad and, eventually, Oslo. Alternatively, take the E20/E4 south of Mälaren, then the E20 to Eskilstuna, meeting the E18 at Arborg.

By bus: There is a reasonable bus service between the bigger towns, but the service to outlying villages is limited. In Uppsala the city buses visit Gamla Uppsala.

There are excellent hotels in all the main towns.

LUXURY

First Hotel Linné, Skolgatan 45, 750 02 Uppsala, tel: 18 102 000, fax: 18 137 597. Best hotel in the area and well-sited close to the Linné museum and gardens. Some rooms overlook the gardens.

Elite Stadshotellet, Kungsgatan 22 651 08 Karlstad, tel: 54 100 200, fax: 54 100 224. Superb 19th-century building which is the best hotel in this part of Sweden. Very comfortable and friendly service.

MID-RANGE

Rica City Hotel Örebro, Kungsgatan 24, 702 24 Örebro, tel: 19 601 4200, fax: 19 601 4209. Simple, but very pleasant hotel of the Rica City chain. Walking distance from the castle.

Scandic Hotel Uppsala, Gamla Uppsalagatan 50, 754 25 Uppsala, tel: 18 495 2300, fax: 18 495 2311. Well placed between 'old' and 'new' Uppsala. Interesting Viking décor. One of the Scandic chain of good-value hotels.

BUDGET

Hotell Storgården, Fredsgatan 11, 703 62 Örebro, tel: 19 120 200, fax: 19 120 255. Just a short walk from the castle. Excellent value.

Karlskoga Hotel, Boåsvägen 2, 691 33 Karlskoga, tel: 58 663 740, fax: 58 663 745. Clean, friendly and good value for money.

All the main towns and villages have excellent restaurants. In the old town centres it is possible to eat in delightful surroundings.

The bigger towns – Uppsala and Västerås in particular, but Eskilstuna, Karlstad and Örebro as well – have reasonable shopping centres. The more outlying towns and villages are good places to look for local crafts for gifts and souvenirs.

The Tourist Information Offices have details of sightseeing tours and excursions. These are limited, usually visiting the major sites – Gamla Uppsala, some of the old mines – but may be worthwhile if you are not driving.

Tourist Information Offices:
Nygatan 15, 631 86 Eskilstuna, tel: 16 107 000, fax: 16 514 575.
Tage Erlandergatan, 652 25 Karlstad, tel: 54 222 140, fax: 54 222 141.
Stora Torget, 611 83 Nyköping, tel: 155 248 200, fax: 155 248 136.
Slottet, 701 35 Örebro, tel: 19 212 121, fax: 19 106 070.
Fyristorg 8, 753 10 Uppsala, tel: 18 274 800, fax: 18 692 477.
Storagatan 40, 722 12 Västerås, tel: 21 103 830, fax: 21 103 850.

4
Southeast Sweden

The southeast of Sweden comprises the regions of Skåne, Blekinge and Småland, and includes one of its major cities. **Malmö**, now linked to Copenhagen by the elegant bridge which crosses the Öresund, is Sweden's third city. It has a fine historical centre surrounded by a modern town where visitors will find excellent shopping and entertainment. Close by is **Lund**, a university town with a famous cathedral, **Trelleborg** with one of Sweden's best Viking sites, and **Helsingborg**, from where Hamlet's Castle can be seen across the sea in Denmark. These sites are in Skåne which was Danish until 350 years ago and still retains a dialect, culture and even architecture which is slightly at odds with the rest of Sweden.

Småland and Blekinge are very different. While Skåne is dotted with towns and villages, these two regions are largely empty, glorious sweeps of forest greeting the visitor who takes the E22 north from Malmö. Some of the towns are linked to Sweden's history – **Karlskrona** with its island fortress, and **Kalmar**, which gave its name to the Union of Scandinavian countries. Today Småland is famous for glass-making and as the birthplace of Astrid Lindgren. Astrid's tales have turned **Vimmerby** into a place of pilgrimage.

North of Småland is Östergötland, which takes in the eastern shore of Vättern, the second largest of Sweden's lakes. Here **Gränna** houses a museum to one of the Arctic's most tragic failures. **Norrköping** has moved seamlessly from old-style industrial to modern service town, using its past in a way which could be an example

Don't Miss

*** **Vadstena:** one of the most beautiful towns in Sweden.
** **Vimmerby:** for anyone who loves the stories of Astrid Lindgren.
** **Lund Cathedral:** particularly for the astronomical clock.
** **Karlskrona:** boat ride to a fascinating fortress.
* **Trelleborg:** reconstructed Viking fort and medieval hut.
* **Ales Stenar:** stunning prehistoric site.

Opposite: *Kalmar Castle, beautifully situated beside a lake and close to the old town.*

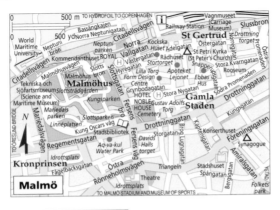

Malmö

TO HYDROFOIL TO COPENHAGEN

to all. It stands close to the Göta Canal, the crossing of which takes the visitor towards Stockholm and the north.

MALMÖ **

Malmö is first mentioned in 1275 when it was probably no more than a fishing village where the fishermen exploited the phenomenally herring-rich waters of Öresund. It is claimed that during the early years of fishing, herring could be scooped out by hand so densely packed were the shoals. The fish, and the well-sheltered harbour, attracted Hanseatic merchants in the early medieval period and their influence can still be seen in St Petri Kyrka with its clear Germanic style. The typical trading ship of the period was the *kogg*, two of which are being built, using authentic tools and method, at **Malmö Kogg** in Norra Neptunigatan to the north of the castle (open 10:00–16:00 daily).

Danish resistance to Hanseatic expansion made Malmö strategically important, particularly after the alliance of the Scandinavian nations – the Kalmar Union. **Malmöhus** (the castle) was built in 1434, the importance of the city indicated by the fact that it housed the Danish royal mint. Under Jörgen Kock, city mayor in the 1520s, the town expanded, Stortorget and some surrounding streets dating from this period of prosperity and expansion. When the Danes lost southern Sweden to the Swedes, Malmö was no longer across the water from the (Danish) capital, but remote from the (Swedish) capital and suffered a decline in its fortunes until the Swedish crown realized its importance in maintaining the security of Öresund. With industrialization, the city rose in importance as a shipbuilding centre: by the early 20th century the Kockums shipyard was one of the world's

---

A FAMOUS PRISONER

James Hepburn was the Earl of Bothwell and husband of Mary, Queen of Scots. When his part in the murder of Lord Darnley, Mary's previous husband, was revealed he fled to Norway. In 1567, Hepburn was captured by the Danes and was imprisoned for six years in the **Malmöhus**. He was then taken to Denmark where he died in 1578.

CLIMATE

The southeast is generally a bit wetter and a bit warmer than Stockholm. Rain can be expected in any month – the rainfall figures for Malmö are remarkably constant. The forests of Småland are wonderful in **spring**, but being **coniferous** do not offer breathtaking autumn colours. Come in **summer** for the beaches. **Winter** can be bleak, but beautiful.

leading shipbuilders. Though its industrial base has been whittled away, Malmö is still a thriving place, seamlessly linking a historic centre with a modern city.

The historic centre is the major visitor attraction. **Stortorget** should be the starting point for an exploratory walk. At its centre is a **statue of King Karl X** who forced the Danes out of Malmö. The square's eastern side is almost filled with the **Rådhuset** (Town Hall), built in 1546, but with a façade remodelled in the 1860s. To its right is **Apoteket Lejonet** (the Lion Pharmacy), founded in 1571 and still operating. The interior, revamped in the 1890s, is delightful. In the diagonally opposite corner is **Kockska Huset**, the home of Mayor Kock.

Leaving the square at the left edge of the Rådhuset the visitor soon reaches **St Petri Kyrka** (St Peter's Church) on Göran Olsgatan, the city's oldest church, built in 1346 in the Germanic 'Baltic-Gothic' style. The early 17th-century four-tiered altar reaches almost 15m (50ft) in height, making it one of the tallest in Europe. Originally the church was extensively decorated, but the murals were whitewashed in the 16th century and totally destroyed in the 1850s. To gain some idea of what the church might have looked like, visit the adjacent **Krämarekapellet** (Merchant's Chapel) which retains its murals.

In the street to the north of the church lies the **St Gertrud area** of the old city. Renovated in fine style, this has some of Malmö's oldest houses, from the 16th century, as well as other splendid buildings from the 17th–19th centuries. At the eastern end of St Gertrud's, in Drottningtorget, is the **Vagnmuseet**, the carriage museum, with a collection of trams, horse-drawn cabs, etc. (open 09:00–16:00 Fri).

South of St Peter's, **Ebbas Hus** – in the unlikely sounding Snapperupsgatan – is Malmö's smallest house, built about 100 years ago and

---

MALMÖHUS

The first castle was built by the Danish King Erik VII in the 1430s. This building, which housed the Danish royal mint for a time, was destroyed in 1534 during civil unrest. It was rebuilt by Christian III in forbidding style in an attempt to cow the locals. After Malmö became Swedish the castle fell into disrepair and was then gutted by fire. What remained was renovated in the 1930s and is now a series of museums – the city museum, city art gallery and the natural history museum which includes an aquarium, reptile house and good nocturnal house.

Below: *Malmö's castle is protected by a formidable moat and embankment.*

Below: *In winter, Malmö's Lilla Torg is transformed into an ice rink.*

furnished in period style (open 12:00–16:00 Wed). A little way east, the **Rooseum** is one of Sweden's best contemporary art galleries, housed in an old power station (open 14:00–20:00 Wed–Fri, 12:00–18:00 Sat, Sun).

At the southwest corner of Stortorget is **Lilla Torg**, a charming 'little square' where the 16th-century houses are now restaurants and galleries. Close by, **Hedmanska Gården**, a beautiful 16th-century courtyard, is now the Form Design Centre showing all that is best in Swedish art and design. Turn right out of Lilla Torg, following Tegelgårdsgatan to Slottsgatan. Cross, with care, to the fine parkland surrounding **Malmöhus** (open 10:00–16:00 daily). To the south from here is **Kronprinsen**, at 52 Regementsgatan, one of Sweden's most famous 1960s buildings. There is a fine view of the city from the restaurant on the 26th floor. (There is another fine view, one which includes the new Öresund bridge, from the **Water Tower** to the south of the city.)

Bear right in the park to cross the Slottsbron bridge – to the right is a boulder inscribed with Stone-Age cup and ring marks – to reach the entrance to Malmöhus and the Science and Maritime Museum. The latter is reached beyond a row of ancient fishermen's huts from which fresh fish is still sold in the morning.

LUND **

In 1990 Lund celebrated the 1000th anniversary of its founding, by Svein Forkbeard in 990 (though some claim a better date would be 1020 when Knud the Great – King Canute of England – made Lund his political and religious centre). The university was founded in 1666 and its influence still dominates the city. IDEON, with over 100 companies, all closely tied to the university, is Scandinavia's biggest research 'village' and helps maintain Lund's Bohemian air and frequent comparisons with Oxford and Yale.

The twin towers of the 12th-century **cathedral** dominate the town. Inside are the famous astronomical clock and, in the crypt, a statue of the giant Finn who, legend has it, built the cathedral. To the north is the delightful **Lundagård Park**. Here, the **Kungshuset** (King's House) was built in the 16th century for the Danish King Frederik II. At the park's eastern edge are the cathedral and history **museums** (open 11:00–16:00 Tue–Fri). Nearby, Tegnér Square is named for Esais

Above: *Joakim Skovgaard's huge mosaic of Christ is a highlight of Lund Cathedral.*

Tegnér (1782–1846), one of Sweden's foremost poets. His house is now a museum. Follow Adelgatan, Lund's most attractive street, passing **Kultiven**, Sweden's biggest and best open-air museum with buildings brought from all over southern Sweden (open 11:00–17:00 daily), to the beautiful **Botanical Gardens**.

South of the cathedral is **Stortorget**, the main square. Further on, the Cathedral School occupies what was the home of King Charles XII from 1716–18. A right turn beyond the school leads to the **City Park** and Lund's excellent **planetarium**.

Finally, head north from Lund to **Höör** where the **Skåne Zoo** has the world's largest collection of Scandinavian animals: 86 species including wolf, musk ox, wolverine and bear. There are play areas for children and a picnic area. Open 10:00–18:00 daily, closes earlier in winter.

LANDSKRONA *

North of Malmö the E6/E20 motorway gives fast access to Landskrona and Helsingborg. Landskrona is an ancient place, but in the 18th century the old town was razed and rebuilt in French style. The **citadellet**, begun in the 16th century but enlarged over the next 200 years, was untouched and remains the best preserved fortress of its era in Scandinavia (guided tours in summer).

PEDAL POWER

To see a different Malmö, borrow a pedalo and explore the canals around the Malmöhus. Children especially will enjoy the tour and there is always a chance of seeing something a little special.

THE ASTRONOMICAL CLOCK

One of Lund Cathedral's great treasures is the 14th-century astronomical clock. At noon (13:00 on Sunday) and 15:00 each day, knights on horseback joust, trumpeters blow a fanfare and *In Dulci Jubilo* plays as the three kings make their way past Mary and the baby Jesus.

HELSINGBORG ★

The strategic importance of **Helsingborg**, set where Öresund is narrowest, has long been recognized, a castle guarding the straits from the 12th century. The city maintained its importance until the Middle Ages when the Danish-Swedish wars caused a spectacular fall from power. Only with industrialization did its position ensure a revival. All that remains of the medieval castle is the 34m (112ft) **Kärnan Tower** on the hill overlooking Stortorget. The surrounding parkland was once occupied by the rest of the castle. Descending the elaborate steps into Stortorget, a right turn into Norra Storgatan takes you to No 21, **Jacob Hansen's House**, the only medieval building to have escaped the destruction of the 17th-century wars. A left turn at the bottom of the steps leads to **St Mary's Church**, the best of the city's churches. In Stortorget, it is hard to ignore the **Rådhuset** (Town Hall) with its 65m (213ft) clock tower.

North of the centre, at **Fredriksdal**, the open-air museum centred on an 18th-century manor house is surrounded by beautiful parkland (open 10:00–20:00 daily Jun–Aug; 11:00–16:00 daily Oct–May). Further north, at **Sofiero**, the summer residence of King Oscar II is famous for the rhododendrons and flower beds. To complete the garden theme, the **Ramlösa Brunnspark**, surrounding 19th-century spa buildings, is also stunning.

From the harbour, ferries cross to **Helsingør** in Denmark, site of Hamlet's Castle, and to **Ven**, the island where Tycho Brahe had his observatory.

THE FAR SOUTH ★

To the east of Malmö, **Torups Slott**, complete with an enclosing moat and walls with towers, is one of the better medieval castles in Scandinavia. Inside there are collections of furniture and paintings. (Open 12:00–17:00 daily.)

TYCHO BRAHE

Considered the greatest astronomer of the pre-telescope era, Tycho Brahe was born in southern Sweden (then under Danish rule) in 1546 and studied mathematics and astronomy at Copenhagen University. He observed a nova in 1572, fixing its position so accurately he could prove it was further away than the moon – an important observation that established his reputation. King Frederick II then funded the building of the Uraniborg (Castle in the Sky) Observatory on the island of Ven. It was here that Brahe's observations showed that the comet of 1577 was more distant than Venus, the first proof that comets were not local phenomena. In 1596 Brahe moved to Prague where he died in 1601. Brahe was an arrogant, short-tempered man who lost most of his nose in a duel while still a student and spent the rest of his life wearing a false nose made of silver.

To the east, near the village of Skurup, **Svaneholm** is an equally impressive 16th-century fortified mansion with similar collections. Open 12:00–16:00 Mon–Fri (until 15:00 Oct–Apr), 13:00–17:00 Sat, Sun.

A much older fortress lies to the south at **Trelleborg**. The fort is one of only two ring fortresses (or *trelleborgs*) discovered in Sweden (both in the south) and one of only six in total, the other four being in Denmark. They are believed to have been constructed by Viking king Harald Bluetooth in the 980s. Originally thought to have been 'barracks' prior to an invasion of Britain, they are now thought to have been the fortified centres of administrative districts, the defences an indication of an enthusiasm for tax collectors which lives on today. A quadrant of the original defensive ring has been reconstructed giving an idea of its original form (viewable at all times). The fort was used after the Vikings departed and one building has been reconstructed to give an idea of how the medieval inhabitants lived. Open 10:00–17:00 daily Jun–Aug.

To the west of Trelleborg at the tiny village of **Kämpinge** there is a fine museum of amber (open 10:00–18:00 daily mid-May to Aug; 11:00–17:00 Sat, Sun Sep to mid-May). The **Falsterbo Peninsula** is one of the main spots in Sweden for finding amber, collectors hunting among the seaweed at low tide. Amber, the hardened resin of ancient pine trees, is fashioned into jewellery and sold in many local shops. Pieces with insects trapped in the resin are most sought after: it was from such a piece that the dinosaurs were created in the film *Jurassic Park*.

East of Trelleborg, **Ystad** is a picturesque town of cobbled streets and half-timbered houses. Ferries leave from here for Bornholm (Denmark's Baltic island) and Swinoujscie in Poland. To see the best of Ystad, follow Stora Östergatan north-east from Stortorget or search out

> ### FALSTERBO'S BIRDS
>
> The Falsterbo Peninsula is important both for breeding birds and for migrating species which use it as a stepping stone on the long journey from northern Scandinavia to southern Europe. Breeding birds include little terns, avocets, bearded tits and Kentish plovers, while one highlight of the migration is seeing flocks of common and honey buzzards soaring above the peninsula before crossing the Baltic to Germany.

Opposite: *From the Kärnan Tower, Helsingborg's skyline is dominated by the Rådhus.*
Below: *A reconstructed medieval hut at the Trelleborg Viking site.*

Stora Norregatan which heads north from St Maria
Kyrka. The church dates from the 14th century and has a
marvellous interior with a fine pulpit and altarpiece.

On the coast east of Ystad lies **Ales Stenar**, Sweden's
largest ship setting (*see* page 14). At nearby **Löderups
Strandbad**, Dag Hammarskjölds Hus was the summer
house of the Swedish secretary general of the United
Nations who was killed in a plane crash in the Congo in
1961. The house is now a museum to his career (open
12:00–17:00 daily Jun–Aug). Hammarskjöld did much to
raise the profile and prestige of the UN, and his death is
still the subject of conspiracy theories.

Heading northeast, **Glimmingehus** is a curiously
shaped five-storeyed castle built in the early 16th century.
The well-preserved castle is bare, but does give an idea
of medieval living. This can be reinforced in the attached
restaurant which serves 'authentic' medieval meals
(open daily, 11:00–17:00 May, 10:00–18:00 Jun–Aug,
11:00–16:00 Sep).

Back on the coast, **Simrishamn** is an attractive little
town, north of which the **Stenshuvud National Park**
was set up to protect the woodland and marshland
which is home to tree frogs and the rare (in Europe)
thrush nightingale. The best of Sweden's Bronze-Age
cairns (*see* page 14) lie a little way north, at **Kivik**.
Heading north from Kivik the visitor reaches **Åhus**
which is famous for its eels (served smoked, with
scrambled eggs in most restaurants).

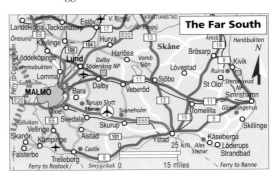

The Far South

KRISTIANSTAD *

Kristianstad is often claimed to be the most Danish town in Sweden, yet it was built by Christian I in 1614 and so was only Danish for 44 years before Denmark lost Skåne to the Swedes. It stood on the border between the hostile states.

The **Bastionen Konungen**, with its earth banks and cannons, is all that remains of the Danish fortress. The rest was levelled, though Christian's street grid was maintained when Kristianstad was rebuilt – the new wide 'boulevards' earning it the name Little Paris. At the edge of the old town – which is enclosed by a delightful canal – the **Trefaldighetskyrkan** (Holy Trinity Church), built by the Danes in 1628 is, by common consent, the finest Renaissance church in Scandinavia. In the centre of the old town the **Filmmuseet** is Sweden's only museum of film, housed in the building where it all began in 1909.

To the east is **Karlshamn**, a lovely little town with some cobbled streets and wooden houses, and also some very grand, late 18th-century houses built by wealthy merchants after a disastrous fire in 1763. Close to the town the huge **Eriksberg Safari Park** has European animals in a beautiful parkland.

Further east, **Ronneby** is another town with a characterful old centre. The **Helga Korskyrkan** (Church of the Holy Cross) has a mural of the *Dance of Death* and gashes in its oak door which are said to date from a battle between Danes and Swedes in September 1564 after which the victorious Swedes slaughtered Danes seeking sanctuary inside.

KARLSKRONA **

Named a World Heritage Site by UNESCO in 1998, Karlskrona and the islands to the south represent one of the finest examples of 17th–18th century naval architec-

Above: *Cannons still wait to repel invaders on the Bastionen Konungen, Kristianstad.*

A JOB FOR THE BRAVE OR TIRELESS

The little window in the tower of Ystad's St Maria Kyrka (St Mary's Church) has been used by the town's nightwatchman from the 17th century when the tower was rebuilt, but was apparently an old tradition even then. The watchman blows a bugle every 15 minutes from 21:15 to 01:00 and in medieval times had his head chopped off if he fell asleep.

Above: *Karlskrona's Stortorget is dominated by the Rådhuset and the statue of King Karl.*

ture in Europe. In 1679 the Danes mounted an (unsuccessful) invasion of Skåne prompting King Karl XI to construct a southern naval base in the ice-free bay behind a line of small offshore islands. The town was built on Trossö Island and from it boat trips can be taken to the **fort** on Tjurkö (ask at the tourist office for details of sailings). The fort has a strange sally-port, a near circular harbour entered through a narrow slot, and impressive buildings and fortifications. The nearby **Drottningskärs Kastell** on Aspö Island was built by master architect Erik Dahlberg and was claimed by Horatio Nelson to make Karlskrona impregnable.

The town is also worth visiting. The huge **Stortorget** has a statue of King Karl, the excellent Rådhuset and two churches: the vast, theatrical Fredrikskyrkan and the Baroque Trefaldighetskyrkan. Behind Fredrikskyrkan, Kyrkagatan (the tourist information office is on the corner) leads to Stumholmen and the town's **Maritime Museum** (open 10:00–18:00 daily Jun–Aug; 11:00–17:00 Tue–Sun Sep–May). Karlskrona's association with the Swedish navy continues, the southern part of the town still being naval property linked to the outside world by a railway which tunnels beneath Stortorget.

Close to the embarkation point for the tours of Karlskrona's fortress is the **Blekinge Museum** housed in a row of houses on Fisktorget, the old fish market street. The museum looks at the old local industries of quarrying and fishing (open 10:00–18:00 daily mid-Jun to mid-Aug; 11:00–17:00 Tue–Sun mid-Aug to mid-June). In a detached part of the museum, in the old Bosun's Barracks on Stumholmen, there is a small art collection. Open 12:00–16:00 Tue–Fri (19:00 Wed), 12:00–17:00 Sat, Sun.

THE MARITIME MUSEUM

Karlskrona's Maritime Museum dates from 1752, making it the oldest in Sweden. The museum is devoted to the history of the Swedish navy and includes an 18th-century shipwreck, a reconstruction of the gundeck of a ship of the line, and several real ships. There is also a collection of figureheads.

KALMAR **

Kalmar was once the third largest city in Sweden and its harbour, sheltered from storms by the island of Öland that lies just 6km (3.8 miles) offshore, was one of the key ports in the Baltic power struggle. In 1397 its castle was the scene of the finalizing of the Kalmar Union, the amalgamation of the three Scandinavian kingdoms into one. Not surprisingly the city is one of the most historically important in Sweden, yet too many potential visitors, intent on getting to the holiday delights of Öland, bypass it.

Medieval Kalmar sat on the mainland, the castle set on a tiny island linked by a defensible causeway. **Gamla Stan**, the old town, is a delight, with cobbled streets and pretty houses, many fronted by colourful shrubs and flowers. The town's **art museum**, with a collection of works by Swedish artists, stands here. Wandering through Gamla Stan the visitor reaches Stadsparken where each summer (dates vary: ask at the tourist information office) the *Medeltida* – a recreation of medieval Kalmar, with craftsmen, archery, jousting and music – takes place.

Beyond the park is **Kalmar Slott**, the famous castle. The first castle may have been built in the 12th century: there was definitely a fortress here a century later, one claimed to be the most impregnable in Sweden. The castle we see today dates from the 16th century when King

> **A DEADLY BROTHER**
>
> The sons of King Gustav Vasa seemed to have raised paranoia to an art form. Johann, the younger, slept in a bed decorated with carved faces – it can still be seen in Kalmar Slott. Fearful that the rightful owners of the bed, which he had stolen, might haunt him, Johann cut off the noses of all the faces, believing the nose was the seat of a man's soul. Johann did not sleep at the castle if his older brother Erik was there. They hated each other and Erik was so convinced that Johann was trying to kill him that he had a secret escape door cut into the panelling of his bedroom. Ultimately Erik (King Erik XIV) died, probably poisoned by arsenic administered by, or on behalf of, his brother who became King Johann III.

Left: *The marina is one of the best spots in the 'new' town of Kalmar.*

A Lucky Escape, A Remarkable Coincidence

When the *Kronan* exploded one sailor, Anders Sparrfelt, was blown over two enemy ships and landed, shocked, but unharmed, in the sail of a Swedish vessel. He was one of only 42 men to survive the catastrophe. In 1980, over 300 years after the disaster, the *Kronan* wreck was finally located by the great-great-great-great-grandson of Admiral Creutz (*see* panel, page 75).

Gustav rebuilt the original as a Renaissance palace. The palace is exquisite – seek out King Erik's chamber to admire the wood panelling and marvel at the kitchen where three whole cows could be roasted simultaneously to satisfy courtly hunger. In the Golden Room, King Erik's portrait hangs higher than the others. It was believed that he was mentally ill (he was certainly paranoiac, but perhaps rightly so) and that the condition could be caught by anyone staring into his (or his portrait's) eyes. Open 10:00–16:00 daily Apr–Sep (until 17:00 Jun–Aug); 10:00–16:00 second weekend of month Oct–Mar.

In **Kvarnholmen**, the new town of Kalmar, there is another collection of fine buildings, watched over by an elaborate water tower (now luxury apartments). The **cathedral**, on Stortorget, is at the new town's heart. It is late 17th century and is claimed by many to be the finest Baroque church in Sweden.

East of the cathedral (technically misnamed as Kalmar does not have a bishop) are two fine museums. The **Sjöfartsmuseum** (Maritime Museum) has a collection of model ships and other sea-based memorabilia, including some very rare items (open 11:00–16:00 Mon–Fri mid-Jun to mid-Sep; 12:00–16:00 Sat, Sun; 12:00–16:00 Sun mid-Sep to mid-June). The **Läns Museum** explores the local history, but is chiefly memorable for its *Kronan* collection (open 10:00–18:00 daily mid-May to mid-Aug; 10:00–16:00 Tue–Fri, 11:00–16:00 Sat, Sun, mid-Aug to mid-May)

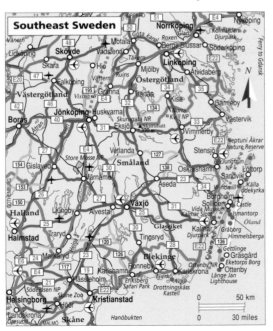

Left: *The Swedes sometimes claim that there are more windmills on Öland than there are in Holland.*

ÖLAND ★★

From Kalmar the Ölandsbron – at 6km (3.8 miles) – the longest bridge in Europe when it was completed in 1972 – links the mainland to **Öland**, an island of beaches and woodland that is popular with sun worshippers and nature lovers. The island has 400 windmills and, it sometimes seems, almost as many camp sites (with prices that are the highest in Sweden).

Borgholm, the island's nominal capital, has one of the island's best-preserved medieval churches, dating from the mid-12th century, but is chiefly famous for **Solliden**, the summer palace of the Swedish royal family, where visitors can enjoy the beautiful palace gardens. Borgholm is also the site of northern Europe's largest ruined castle. Built in medieval times, the castle was partially destroyed in 1617. The royal intention to restore it as a palace was defeated by lack of cash, and fire finally ruined it.

North of Borgholm, **Sandvik** has what is sometimes claimed to be the largest Dutch windmill in the world. North again, the tip of the island should be visited not only for the **Neptuni Åkrar Nature Reserve** (famous for its viper's bugloss, a sturdy plant with bright blue flowers) but also for a Viking burial field. On the east coast, **Källa ödekyrka** is a ruined fortified church, built in medieval times as a refuge from pirates.

> **THE KRONAN**
>
> In 1676 the *Kronan*, twice the size of the *Vasa* and one of the largest warships afloat, was leading an attempt to recapture Gotland from the Danish. Close to Öland, after a skirmish with a Danish/Dutch fleet, the *Kronan's* captain, Admiral Lorentz Creutz (a very inexperienced sailor despite his rank), decided to fight again, undeterred by warnings from his more experienced officers that the wind was wrong for a turning manoeuvre. As the *Kronan* turned, the wind took the ship. It heeled over, and water flooding through the open gun ports caused the list to increase so that a lantern fell off its hook. It ignited the powder magazine and the ship exploded, killing 800 sailors. Although some relics (now in Kalmar's Länsmuseum) were salvaged from the ship, there was no hope of salvaging the ship itself – the explosion had ripped her apart.

South of Borgholm at **Halltorp**, the Vida Museum, opened in 2001, is an exciting contemporary art gallery concentrating on post-1960 work. Open 09:00–17:00 daily May–Sep (19:00 Jun–Aug); 10:00–17:00 Sat, Sun Oct–Apr. Further south, the **Djurpark** is the island zoo, with the usual collection of animals and an amusement park with model dinosaurs (open 10:00–18:00 daily May–Aug). Across the island **Himmelsberga** is Öland's main museum, the collection of buildings representing a history of island life and culture over the centuries (open 10:00–18:00 May–Aug). Inland of the village/museum site, **Ismantorp** is an abandoned fortress/village. Heading south, **Gräsgård** should be visited, though it will take little time to enjoy the delights of this tiny fishing hamlet.

Not far away, **Eketorps Borg** is a marvellous recon-structed fortress. The site is original (and was excav-ated in the 1960s) but the wall and buildings within it have been constructed to give an idea of how life was lived in the Iron Age, Viking and early medieval periods when the fortress was occupied. Craftsmen in period dress enhance the scene, while a museum holds the best of the excavated finds. Open 10:00–17:00 daily May–Sep.

At the southern tip of Öland the lighthouse of **Långe Jan** is, at 42m (138ft), the tallest in Sweden. There is a picnic room at the light. Nearby, the **Ottenby Nature Reserve** is one of Öland's best for bird-watching. Interested visitors can make use of pur-pose-built watchtowers and also follow waymarked trails. At the village of **Ottenby** there is a museum (Vogelmuseum) dedicated to the area's breeding and migrating bird species. Open 10:00–16:00 daily May–Sep, 11:00–15:00 Sat, Sun Oct–Apr.

Finally, head north again to visit two of Öland's most important prehistoric sites. At **Gettlinge** there are over 250 Bronze- and Iron-Age graves including stone settings, while at **Gråborg** there is a huge Iron-Age ring fort. Close to Gråborg, the ruined St Knud's Chapel dates from about 1200.

GLASRIKET *

Inland of Kalmar is **Glasriket**, the Kingdom of Crystal, so called because it is the centre of the Swedish glass-making industry. All forms of glass, from humble tumblers to exquisite works of art, are made here. In all there are 15 glassworks in which visitors can watch the process, including the work of some of the world's most skilled glassblowers, and buy the finished products at much cheaper prices than elsewhere. There are also numerous museums which explore the history and culture of the industry. Many of these are allied to the glass-making centres, but for a good overview the museum in Växjö is excellent.

Even those not particularly interested in glass or glass-making will find a visit to Glasriket worthwhile. With its thick forests and picturesque villages of red houses it is no surprise that after Stockholm and Gothenburg this is the most visited area of Sweden.

Växjö, birthplace of tennis star Mats Wilander, is the main city of the area though technically it lies outside Glasriket. The city has a fine cathedral, reputedly built on the site of a wooden church erected by St Sigfrid who came from York, England, in the 11th century to convert the Swedes. The building, with its twin copper-clad spires, has a history of lightning strikes and fires so that almost nothing remains of the 15th-century original. The town has an interesting museum – Utvandrarnas Hus, Emigrant House – which contains information on Swedes who emigrated to the USA. Many Americans of Swedish descent come from this area, and often return to delve into the museum's historical archive.

GLASRIKET

It is not possible here to give a comprehensive outline of the specialities of the 15 major glass-making factories of Glasriket. A leaflet, available from all local tourist offices, does this, and includes a map showing the location of each company. Visitors wanting to try just one or two sites should consider **Kosta**, where it all began in the mid-18th century, **Orrefors**, the most famous, and **Afors**, a personal favourite.

Below: *Decorative glassware in Glasriket.*

NORTH SMÅLAND *

North of Kalmar the E22 takes the visitor through exquisite wooded country enlivened by the possibility that the elks shown on the frequent 'Beware of the Elk' signs might actually appear. **Oskarshamn** has a maritime museum and another of the woodcarvings of Axel Petersson. Known as the *Döderhultern*, Petersson's work recreates late 19th-century Småland. The curious name derives from that of the local area (Döderhult), and those wishing to see Petersson's Döderhult should visit **Stensjö**, a village north of Oskarshamn, which is as it was in his time.

VÄSTERVIK *

The E22 now hurries visitors on to **Västervik**, birthplace of the tennis player Stefan Edberg and the place where Abba's Björn Ullvaeus grew up. The town, popular with holiday-makers and sailors, has two fine churches. On the southern side the glorious St Petri Kyrka is a miniature cathedral, while to the north St Gertruds is altogether more modest. Much older, St Gertruds has an octagonal clock tower and, inside, one of Sweden's most valuable organs. Close to St Peter's, **Båtmansgränd** (Ferrymen Alley) is a series of eight interlocking log cabins built in the 18th century for local ferrymen. From the cabins a walk along the seafront takes you to the tourist office, housed in the superb Art-Nouveau bathhouse of 1910. From the office there is a view to the ruins

Below: *The delightful harbour at Västervik.*

of the castle which once protected the entrance to Västervik harbour. From the tourist office, continue around the harbour to reach St Gertruds Church near which there are beautiful old houses, particularly **Aspagården**, at No. 9 Västra Kyrkagatan, built in 1677 and so the town's oldest house.

Vimmerby **

Inland of Västervik is **Vimmerby**, famous as the birth-place of Astrid Lindgren, Sweden's most famous author (though the literary establishment gets a little sniffy about her credentials, her children's books not being serious enough to be taken seriously). The town has a very good museum, the **Näktergalen** (Nightingale), with excavated finds from a Viking graveyard and other inter-esting items in an 18th-century building with an interior decorated in Baroque style (open 11:00–17:00 Mon–Fri, 10:00–14:00 Sat, Sun, mid-June to mid-Aug), but that, and the very pleasant old streets, lose out to Astrid fever. Astrid's birthplace, the Bullerbyn (a row of houses that inspired stories of the Bullerby children), and Emil's Katthult (named for Emil, her other famous creation) can be visited, but most visitors make for **Astrid Lindgren's World** to be beguiled by a young lady dressed as Pippi – complete with improbable pigtails – and to enjoy the theme park (open 10:00–18:00 daily May–Sep).

Eksjö *

West of Vimmerby, **Eksjö** is a contrast to the hectic activity of Pippi-seeking, a quiet town that is a centre for walkers enjoying the lovely Småland countryside. The **Skurugata Nature Reserve**, to the northeast, is one excellent spot, the climb to the top of **Skuruhatt** – a 320m (1000ft) hill – offering wonderful views. In the town, exploring north of Stortorget is worthwhile, as is a visit to the town museum (open 08:00–20:00 daily mid-Jun to mid-Aug; 13:00–18:00 Tue–Fri, 12:00–16:00 Sat, Sun, mid-Aug to mid-June).

Norrköping *

Continuing north through more beautiful country, the visitor reaches **Söderköping**, where the Göta Canal is crossed, and **Norrköping**, a prosperous 18th-century textile-making centre which has built on its industrial past to become a modern centre with museums, event and conference centres, a concert hall and a research centre. With its weir waterfall, bridges and walkways

Above: *The weir at Norrköping's reclaimed industrial heritage site.*

the area is an absolute delight, and a real contrast to some cities where the post-industrial age has led to decay and eyesore ruins. The area's **Stadsmuseum** explores the town's past (open 10:00–17:00 Tue, Wed, Fri, 10:00–22:00 Thu, 11:00–17:00 Sat, Sun), while the **Arbetets Museum** is devoted to work – its industrial history, varying conditions and modern ethos. Open 11:00–17:00 Mon–Sun (until 20:00 on Tue). The restaurant and café in the centre are excellent, with great views. On the western outskirts of the town there is a museum of the important collection of Bronze-Age rock carvings found in the valley of the Motala River. Open 11:00–16:00 daily May–Aug (until 18:00 in July).

LINKÖPING ★

Southwest of Norrköping, **Linköping** was the scene of the decisive battle of Sweden's religious wars, a Protestant army defeating the Catholic army of the Polish King Sigismund to win a control that they still maintain. Many Catholic leaders were executed in the town. Ironically, Linköping is now famous for its cathedral, a vast building with a 107m (350ft) spire.

To the west of the city **Gamla Linköping** is Sweden's largest village/museum – very quaint and worthwhile – with about 60 19th-century buildings, some housing small museums (times vary: ask at the tourist office). Nearby there are several other museums (of railways, of carriages and one of electricity production) and a very good children's play area. Also to the west is the **Swedish Royal Air Force Museum** with a collection of military aircraft spanning the years from its inception in 1911 to the present (open 10:00–17:00 daily Jun–Aug; 12:00–16:00 Tue–Sun Sep–May).

KOLMÅRDEN

Close to Norrköping, **Kolmården Djurpark** claims to be Europe's biggest zoo, with over 1000 animals distributed through a safari park, a dolphinarium and a tropical house with reptiles and spiders. There is also a children's zoo and play area, and refreshments varying from fast food to excellent restaurant cuisine. Open 10:00–17:00 daily May, 09:00–18:00 daily Jun–Aug, 10:00–17:00 Sat, Sun Sep.

EAST OF LAKE VÄTTERN ★★★

Northwest of Linköping, at **Bergs Slussar**, is one of the most picturesque sections of the Göta Canal where the seven locks of Carl Johan Locke take it into Lake Roxen. To the west is **Vadstena**, a lovely town in a beautiful setting by the equally attractive lake of Vättern. The town was once a religious centre, a monastery having been built here by St Birgitta (Sweden's first female saint) in the 14th century. The abbey church houses the saint's relics and the cobbled streets between it and the main square are an absolute joy. Vadstena was also a royal centre, the castle by the lake having been built by Gustav Vasa and embellished by his son Johann III. Abandoned in 1716 the castle then served as a granary, but has now been restored. Part serves as a repository for regional records, but most is open to visitors. Open 11:00–15:00 Mon–Fri May; 10:00–18:00 daily Jun–Aug (until 19:00 in Jul); 10:00–14:00 Mon–Fri Sep–Apr.

Very different from the castle is the town's hospital museum. This was Sweden's oldest mental hospital and some of the exhibits are more terrifying than those found in the Chamber of Horrors of most waxworks. Exhibits include spinning chairs intended to induce vomiting and baths of electric eels for 'difficult' patients – hardly holiday fare, but a real eye-opener (open 13:00–15:00 daily Jul). Next door is the less disturbing Mårten Skinnores Hus. Skinnores was a rich 16th-century merchant whose house had all mod cons including an indoor toilet (no flush, just a hole above the pig sty in the yard below).

The area close to Vadstena is as pretty as the town, particularly the country to the south around **Lake Tåkern** which is a nature reserve known for its bird life. There is an observation tower close to the church of **Väversunda** which is a strange-looking place with interesting medieval murals.

> ### St Birgitta
>
> Married at 13, Birgitta (1303–1373), a royal lady-in-waiting, had eight children in not many more years and then, perhaps not surprisingly, had a vision that she should take holy orders. After convincing her royal employers to agree to, and fund, the monastery at Vadstena, Birgitta travelled to Rome to obtain Papal approval. The Pope was in Avignon and Birgitta spent several years campaigning for his return. She succeeded, but died before returning to Vadstena, work there continuing under her daughter Katarina. Birgitta was canonized in 1391.

Below: *A yacht passes a modern drawbridge on the Göta Canal.*

Southeast Sweden at a Glance

BEST TIMES TO VISIT

Öland should be visited in summer. This is also the best time for Glasriket and most of the other visitor sites in the area. Spring is also lovely in Glasriket, and autumn can be if the weather is fine. Winter is cold and can be bleak.

GETTING THERE

By air: There are direct flights to Malmö from many European cities, and internal flights to the city from Stockholm. There are also airports at Helsingborg, Kalmar, Linköping, Norrköping and Växjö.
By train: A good service links the main towns of the area to Malmö and Stockholm.
By road: The Öresund link makes it easy to reach Malmö from Copenhagen (and, therefore, the European motorway system). The **E22** (see page 48) links Malmö with Stockholm passing close to, or through, many of the main towns of the area which tend to be coastal.
By ferry: Malmö, Trelleborg and Ystad are linked by ferry to Poland and Germany.

GETTING AROUND

By bus: There is a reasonable bus service between the main towns, but services to the villages are more limited.
By road: The roads are good and access by car is easy.

WHERE TO STAY

The range of accommodation for visitors to Sweden is excel-
lent. Malmö has very pleasant hotels (and a wide range of them) and the other main towns also offer good opportunities. The local Tourist Offices usually have lists, and will offer a booking service.

LUXURY
Hotel Noble House, Gustav Adolfs Torg 47, 211 22 Malmö, tel: 40 664 3000, fax: 40 664 3050. Apparently named by a previous owner for the James Clavell novel, the owner being a big fan. In the big square to the south of Stortorget (the main square). Excellent facilities.

Romantik Slottshotellet, Slottsvägen 7, 392 23 Kalmar, tel: 480 88260, fax: 480 88266. In the centre of the old town, therefore close to the castle and main museums. Beautifully furnished in an old-fashioned, but delightful, way. Absolutely first-class.

Vadstena Klosterhotel, Klosterområdet, 592 24 Vadstena, tel: 143 31530, fax: 143 13648. Housed in a 12th-century convent, the most romantic hotel in a beautiful city. Understated, but superb, rooms. Excellent service.

MID-RANGE
Rica City Hotel Malmö, Stortorget 15, 211 22 Malmö, tel: 40 660 9550, fax: 40 660 9559. In the main square, which is good for sightseeing,
but awkward for parking as there is no car park and the square fills quickly. Pleasant decor and good service.

Elite Hotel Mollberg, Stortorget 18, Box 1476, 251 14 Helsingborg, tel: 42 373 7000, fax: 42 373 737. The site dates back to the 14th century (and underlines the claim to its being the oldest hotel in Sweden) though the building is 19th century. Very atmospheric, and nicely positioned.

Vimmerby Stadshotell, Sevedegatan 39, 598 37 Vimmerby, tel: 492 12100, fax: 492 14643. The ideal place if spending time with Pippi Longstocking and friends or exploring Glasriket.

BUDGET
Hotell Royal, Norra Vallgatan 94, 211 22 Malmö, tel: 40 664 2500, fax: 40 127 712. Three old buildings by the canal knocked into one to form a well-positioned, inexpensive hotel of some charm. No restaurant, but close to the main city eateries.

ProNova Hotell & Konferens, Norra Grystgatan 10, 601 86 Norrköping, tel: 11 442 4520, fax: 11 187 606. Close to the Industrial Centre and the other main city sites. Inexpensive but very pleasant.

Hotell Siesta, Borgmästaregatan 5, 371 31 Karlskrona,

Southeast Sweden at a Glance

tel: 455 80180, fax: 455 80182. Quiet and comfortable hotel close to both the main square and the harbour for boats to the fortress.

Where to Eat

All the main towns have excellent restaurants, the coastal ones often specializing in seafood. Worth a try are:

Staket, Stora Södergatan 6, 222 24 Lund, Tel: 46 211 9367. The curious façade of this mid-16th century building is one of the landmarks of Lund. The menu offers delicious fish and meat dishes. Excellent fondue is served in the basement.

Årstiderna Kockska Huset, Frans Suellsgatan 3, 201 21 Malmö, tel: 40 230 910. One of the best restaurants in southern Sweden, housed in vaulted cellar of the home of 15th-century Mayor Jörgen Kock on the corner of Stortorget. Superb menu and service. Booking recommended.

In Malmö there are also several very good restaurants in Lilla Torg where it is possible to eat on the square.

Rådhuskälleren, Rådhustorget, 592 30 Vadstena, tel: 143 12170. Housed in the cellar of the oldest town hall/courthouse in Sweden. Extremely atmospheric. Excellent menu of meat

and fish dishes. If it's on the dessert menu, try the elderflower ice cream.

Shopping

In Malmö the main shopping area, a pedestrianized area, runs south along Södergatan from Stortorget to Gustav Adolfs Torg, and then along Södra Förstadsgatan. Hansa Companiet, at Stora Nygatan 50, is a complex of about 40 shops ranging from fashion to gift suggestions. For beautifully crafted souvenirs, try the Form Design Centre in Lilla Torg. The other main towns also have good shopping areas – Helsingborg is particularly good. Kullagatan was the first pedestrianized shopping street in Sweden and is still a good place to start. Stortorget is also worth a look. Outside the main towns the chief shopping opportunity is Glasriket with its wealth of glass shops. Most factory outlets sell glassware much cheaper than it can be obtained elsewhere, and this is especially true if 'seconds' are bought. Invariably the flaws which make them seconds are undetectable to the untrained eye.

Tours and Excursions

The Tourist Information Office has details of numerous tours of Malmö and excursions to local sites of interest. Trips run from Malmö to Lund and Helsingborg, and also to some of the more specialist sites

(such as Trelleborg). A great trip is a pedal boat around the Malmö canals.

Useful Contacts

Tourist Information Offices:
Sandgatan 21, 387 21 Borgholm, tel: 485 89000, fax: 485 89010.
Södra Storgatan 1, 251 21 Helsingborg, tel: 42 104 350, fax: 42 104 355.
Larmgatan 6, Box 23, 391 20 Kalmar, tel: 480 15350, fax: 480 17453.
Stortorget, 371 21 Karlskrona, tel: 455 303 490, fax: 455 303 494.
Stora Torg, 291 32 Kristianstad, tel: 44 121 988, fax: 44 120 898.
Engelbrecksgatan 11, 582 21 Linköping, tel: 13 127 180, fax: 13 127 184.
Kyrkagatan 11, 222 22 Lund, tel: 46 355 040, fax: 46 125 963.
Central Station, 211 20 Malmö, tel: 40 341 200, fax: 40 341 209.
Dalsgatan 16, 601 81 Norrköping, tel: 11 155 000, fax: 11 155 074.
Vadstena Slott, 592 80 Vadstena, tel: 143 31572, fax: 143 31579.
Strömsholmen, 593 30 Västervik, tel: 490 88900, fax: 490 88915.
Västra Tullportsgatan 3, Box 3, 598 21 Vimmerby, tel: 492 31010, fax: 492 13065.
Skt Knuds Torg, 271 42 Ystad, tel: 411 577 681, fax: 411 555 585.

5
Gotland

L ying almost halfway between southern Sweden and Latvia, and the largest of all Baltic islands, Gotland is more than just a place for an excursion from the mainland. With its mix of beautiful and varied scenery and historically important sites, it is a worthy destination. Many visitors who go for a short trip find that they are reluctant to leave or that their stay has eaten into their time in a way that they had not contemplated.

Visby, the island's 'capital', is a UNESCO World Heritage Site, a virtually intact walled medieval town and port. Visby is where visitors arrive by sea or air, and is a good base for exploring the island. More adventurous visitors can take advantage of the freedom to camp and the fact that the essentially flat landscape – the highest point is only 81m (265ft) above sea level – is ideal for exploration on foot or by bicycle. As well as interesting sites, the island also has some excellent beaches and a range of fascinating events so that families will find it as worthwhile a destination as cyclists and walkers.

Northern Gotland is rugged, the wild scenery reaching a crescendo on the island of **Fårö** with its sea stacks. The north also has the caves of **Lummelunda**, an equally exciting example of rock architecture. Southern Gotland has, by contrast, a gentler landscape, lush farmland replacing the wildness, although there is another famous sea stack off the southern tip. The eastern part of the island is different again, with many ancient sites and a beautiful coastline (though the tourist office brochure which suggests an archipelago is a clear tongue-in-cheek description of the

Opposite: *Visby is one of Europe's best preserved medieval cities.*

Below: *Though the medieval walls are the main attraction, there is much more to Visby.*

handful of small offshore islands). The fishing villages of the east coast are wonderfully picturesque.

VISBY **

In Viking times Gotland was a natural stepping stone for expeditions across the Baltic. With the decline in influence of the Vikings the islanders were freed from mainland control and began to prosper as an independent trading nation. By the 12th century, Gotland was signing treaties and exchanging ambassadors with European states, but its independence attracted the interest of the Hanseatic League. Hanseatic merchants moved in, their arrival increasing Gotland's prosperity, but making it vulnerable to attack by the League's enemies. Visby, the major port, was protected by a huge wall in the 13th century, but this was actually built to keep the locals away from the merchants, rather than to keep invaders out. When the Danish King Valdemar attacked in 1361 his army slaughtered several thousand islanders: only then did the merchants surrender the town. Valdemar had part of the wall knocked down so that he could ride into the town in triumph. It was not until 1645 that the Swedes wrested Gotland from Danish rule.

The **town wall**, with its 40 towers, is the prominent feature of Visby. The wall is broken in only two places and so gives a marvellous idea of how a medieval town looked, particularly as cars are excluded from within it during the summer. A stroll around the narrow, cobbled Visby streets is a delight. The ruins of 10 medieval churches stand within the walls, these including **Helge And Kyrka**, which is the only octagonal stone church in Sweden. One complete church is the **Domkyrkan** (cathedral). It dates from the early 13th century, but required refurbishment after four serious

fires. Inside, look for the curious row of grotesque faces beneath the pulpit.

South of the cathedral, the best of the old merchant houses are in **Strandgatan**. Here, too, is the **Gotlands Fornsal**, a museum focusing on the island's history. Of particular interest are the picture stones. The later stones, from the Viking age, have runic inscriptions, but some are much older and carved with animals, people, ships and houses (open 12:00–17:00 daily May to mid-Sep). The town also has a good art museum, a natural history museum and a collection of old cars, motorcycles and tractors.

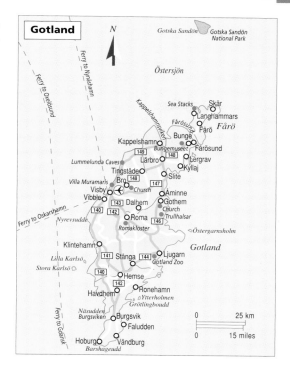

THE ISLAND ★★★

North of Visby, on road 149, the **Villa Muramaris**, once the home of an art professor, is the venue for art exhibitions and stands in a fine Baroque garden (open 12:00–18:00 daily Jun to mid-Aug). Inland from this, the church at **Bro** is one of the island's most beautiful. Inside are several picture stones dated to the 5th century and some exquisite sculptures.

Back on the coast road (No. 149) visitors soon reach **Lummelunda** where there are caves etched into the limestone by aeons of water activity. The first cavern was used in Stone-Age times, but not until the 1950s when intrepid local boys penetrated further was it realized that the cavern was merely the opening to an extensive system. The show cave, only a fraction of

---

BE A VIKING FOR A DAY

A little way south of Visby the **Vikingabyn** gives visitors the opportunity not only to watch craftsmen at work on the old Viking crafts, but to join in. Try your hand at spinning Gute sheep wool, baking bread on an open fire, grinding flour the old way, or throwing a spear. There are also mock battles and storytellers recounting the deeds of Viking heroes. (Open 10:00–17:00 daily mid-June to mid-Aug.)

Above: : *Fårö Island, off Gotland's northern shore, is famous for its sea stacks.*

FÅRÖ AND GOTSKA SANDÖN

Fårö (Sheep Island) lies off Gotland's northern coast and is famed for its limestone heathland and the fabulous sea stacks at Langhammars and Lauterhorn. Many writers have extolled the delight of watching the sun set beyond the stacks, but watching it rise is far superior. **Gotska Sandön**, a triangular island, also lies off Gotland's north coast. Despite being very isolated it has been occupied since Stone-Age times. Today it is a national park, set up to protect sand dunes, forests of wind-gnarled pines, heather and lichens.

---

the explored length, has beautiful stalagmites and stalactites. The more adventurous can join a trip beyond the show cave (open 10:00–17:00 daily May to mid-Sep).

Heading north from Bro, road 148 reaches **Lärbro**. Until recently access beyond here was difficult because of military activity, but restrictions have been relaxed, allowing visitors to reach **Bunge** where an open-air museum explores Gotland life in the 17th–19th centuries (open 10:00–18:00 daily Jul to mid-Aug). Visitors can now continue even further and explore the northern coast and the island of **Fårö**.

Inland of Visby, at **Dalhem**, steam engines still haul trains along an old section of line during the summer months. There is also a railway museum. Further east, there is a fine church at **Gothem**, and, close by, a number of standing stones from the Bronze Age. South of Dalhem, at **Roma**, the old abbey is the setting for summer plays, including atmospheric versions of Shakespeare. At **Ljugarn**, the Gotland Zoo has about 40 species and, interestingly, also includes several prehistoric sites within its boundaries (open 10:00–17:00 daily May–Aug).

Continue along road 144 inland to **Stånga** which has an exquisite 14th-century church. The southern tip of the island can be reached, but has nothing to compare to the rock architecture of the north. Rather head to the west coast for a trip to either of the **Karlsö** islands, which are both nature reserves. **Lilla Karlsö** has wave-carved cliffs and sea stacks, and is home to Gute sheep – the unique Gotland horned sheep. It is also the breeding place for countless auks, and for peregrine falcons. **Stora Karlsö** is also home to sea-bird colonies, but has a more varied scenery, with moorland, flower meadows and small woods.

Gotland at a Glance

Summer on Gotland is by far the best season, though bird-watchers will enjoy the sea cliff bird colonies in spring. Clear autumn days are a delight. Winter can be cold and windy, but even then Visby is lovely.

By air: There is an airport at Visby with regular domestic flights (operated by Skyways) from Stockholm and Norrköping, and also a number of international flights from European cities. **By ferry:** Ferries cross to Visby from Oskarshamn and Nynäshamn. The regular ferries take 4hr from Oskarshamn and 5hr from Nynäshamn. A new high-speed ferry, also on the Nynäshamn-Visby route, takes 3hr. All ferries carry passengers and cars.

Bicycles are the best way, but there is also a limited bus service. The roads are excellent but be careful of cyclists.

LUXURY
Wisby Hotel, Strandgatan 6, Box 1319, 621 24 Visby, tel: 498 257 500, fax: 498 257 550. The best hotel on the island; housed in a building with medieval ancestry. Well sited and well appointed. Rooms drop in price in winter.
Strand Hotel, Strandgatan 34, 621 56 Visby, tel: 498 258

800, fax: 498 258 811. A Best Western hotel. Very comfortable; well sited and well appointed; much cheaper out of season.

MID-RANGE
Hotell Gute, Mellangatan 29, 621 56 Visby, tel: 498 202 260, fax: 498 202 262. Excellent, family-run hotel with very good facilities.

Hotel St Clements, Smedje-gatan 3, 621 55 Visby, tel: 498 219 000, fax: 498 279 443. Inside the city wall; set in beautiful gardens. Friendly service and good facilities.

BUDGET
Suderbys Herrgård, Väster-hejde, 621 99 Visby, tel: 498 296 030, fax: 498 264 867. Extremely pleasant atmosphere and set in lovely grounds. Rooms are in a new wing added to an older mansion.

Katthamra Gård, Katt-hammarsvik, 620 16 Ljugarn, tel/fax: 498 52009. Comfortable budget line accommodation out of Visby. Washbasins in rooms, but shared toilet and bath. Excellent service.

There are excellent restaurants in Visby, and good ones in island villages too.

Koggen, Färjeleden 3, 621 58 Visby, tel: 498 201 262. Close to the ferry. Very

atmospheric in renovated building. Family run. Good menu. Serves breakfast from 06:00. Part of the 'Culinary Gotland' chain.

Gutekälleren, Stortorget 3, 621 28 Visby, tel: 498 210 043. Delightful restaurant in one of the oldest buildings in town. Excellent menu and service.

Sjökrogen, Vallevikenshamn, 620 34 Lärbro, tel: 498 223 015. Very pleasant harbour setting. Excellent menu and cooking. Part of the 'Culinary Gotland' chain.

Apart from craft outlets in the larger island villages, shopping means Visby where handcrafts are the most popular items. Gotlands Fornsal sells replicas of some museum pieces.

Visby's Tourist Information Office has details of excursions to the islands. Many people come to the island without transport so there are some good opportunities for visiting the out-of-town sites.

Gotlands Turistservice, Österväg 3A, 621 45 Visby, tel: 498 203 300, fax: 498 203 390.
Skyways, Visby Airport, tel: 20 959 500.
Destination Gotland (Ferry company), tel: 498 201 020.

6
Southwest
Sweden

A thousand years ago, when southern Sweden was part of Denmark, Svealand and Norrland, the kingdoms that lay north of the Danish holding, joined with Götaland to create Sweden. As with the other areas of medieval Sweden Götaland, named for the Göta älv, the Göta River, has maintained its ancient name and borders as a region of modern Sweden.

Götaland is the most scenically diverse of Swedish regions. North of Gothenburg lies **Bohuslän**, an area with a beautiful, jagged coastline. Here some of the deeply incut fjords shelter equally beautiful old fishing villages. Inland, Bronze-Age carvings speak of a landscape which has supported man for millennia. North of Bohuslän, **Dalsland** is quite different, with areas of forest and numerous lakes. On the western edge Dalsland borders Norway. On the east it reaches the shore of the vast **Vänern Lake**. **Gothenburg** is Sweden's second city and its major industrial centre. It is also a fascinating place with some of the country's best museums and galleries, one of Sweden's amusement parks, and some of its finest parks and gardens.

To the east of Gothenburg, **Västergötland** is squeezed between Sweden's two great lakes. There are interesting towns here – **Lidköping** and **Jönköping** – while near the southern edge of Vättern, **Gränna** is associated with one of the Arctic's most tragic tales. The area is crossed by the **Göta Canal**, one of Europe's great waterways: the Swedes often suggest that the canal is a linear national park. Götaland also includes **Östergötland**, east of

Don't Miss

*** **Gothenburg Konst-museet:** terrific collection by Scandinavian and other European artists.
** **Göta Canal:** Sweden's 'linear national park'.
** **Lisebergs:** Sweden's best amusement park.
** **Gränna:** extraordinary display of material from a doomed Arctic venture.
** **Hornborgasjön:** for its dancing cranes.
* **Åstol and Smögen:** very picturesque fishing villages.
* **Ekornavallen:** atmospheric prehistoric site.

Opposite: *Gothenburg's Trädgårdsföreningens (Horticultural Park) is one of the city's best-known features.*

Right: *Boarding a boat for a trip along Gothenburg's canals.*

Vättern, already explored in the Southeast Sweden chapter. Finally, it includes **Halland**, south of Gothenburg, an area of excellent beaches and fine old towns, particularly **Falkenberg** and **Halmstad**.

GOTHENBURG (GÖTEBORG) ★★★

Although there were fishing villages in the coastal area close to where the Göta älv reached the Kattegatt there was no big town, the area being protected by the fort of Älvsborg built at the mouth of the river. The decision not to improve the Swedish grip on the area is curious. The Danes held the land to the south, and to the north they also held Norway and parts of Dalsland and Bohuslän. The Göta River was Sweden's only link to the North Sea, yet the frequent incursions of Danes did not provoke the reaction that might have been anticipated. Not until 1619, that is. In 1612 the Danes took Älvsborg and demanded a ransom so vast for its return that it took Sweden seven years to accumulate the cash. When they had finally retrieved their fort, King Gustav Adolf visited the area. It is said that, fed up with constant Danish aggression and the drain on the royal purse, he rode up Stora Otterhällan Hill and, pointing towards an area of meadowland, declared that a new town would be built there, one that would be properly defended. In Gustav Adolfs Torg, in front of Gothenburg's Rådhuset (Town Hall), the king's gesture is captured in bronze.

The new town was largely the work of the Dutch, brought in for their expertise in draining swamps and in the hope that they would use the port they built to export Swedish timber and iron and so help fund the project. Many of the canals the Dutch built have been filled, but those that still exist are a delightful feature of the city. Gothenburg rapidly grew to become a major port. When the Swedish East India Company was established in the late 18th century (by a Scot, Colin Campbell) its trade with China, from Gothenburg was actually worth more than the Swedish national budget. Such incredible wealth was bound to bring in other industries: shipbuilding was first, then textiles, the latter spawning the ball-bearing industry (*see* panel, page 95) that itself led to car production and the birth of Volvo. SKF and Volvo (now part of Ford) are still here, as are Hasselblad and the space technology part of the Saab-Ericsson group. Both Volvo and Hasselblad have museums to the development of their products.

A good place to start an exploration of the city is **Götaplatsen** at the top of Kungsportsavenyn. The square is dominated by the 7m (23ft) statue of **Poseidon** by Carl Milles, Sweden's most famous sculptor. When it was first unveiled in 1931 the god's 'maleness' caused offence because of its proportions and a reduction was required – or so it is said. In the square are the city's theatre and concert hall and the **Konstmuseet**, the excellent art museum which has work by leading Scandinavian artists (including Munch and Zorn) as well as such greats as Chagall, Picasso and Rembrandt.

From the square take **Kungsportsavenyn**, (usually just 'Avenyn' to the

> ### THE 1660 RIKSDAG
>
> In 1659 King Karl X Gustav summoned a *riksdag* (parliament) as he needed to raise money for his continuing campaign against the Danes. The king decided to hold it in Gothenburg, a sure sign of the new town's growing importance in Sweden. On 4 January 1660 he opened the parliament in the Kronhuset, but soon retired with a cough. Over the next few days the king had trouble breathing and finally, after a month of increasingly poor health, he died in the Residenset in Södra Hamngatan. His four-year-old son was immediately taken to the Kronhuset to be acclaimed King Karl XI.

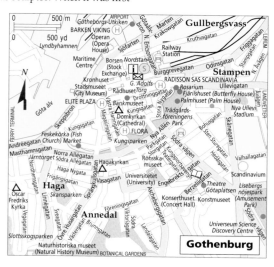

THE THIRD KING

The statue of King Gustav Adolf was commissioned in 1845. The first bronze casting (in Rome) was so poor that another was ordered. This, cast in Munich, was perfect, but the ship carrying it to Gothenburg sank off Heligoland. The statue was rescued by German fishermen, but the salvage price they asked was so extortionate that a third statue was cast. That is the one we see. The second mouldered away in Bremen until 1942 when it was melted down to help the German war machine.

Below: *Milles' statue of Poseidon in Götaplatsen has become a symbol of Gothenburg.*

locals), the city's most fashionable street with the best restaurants and clubs. At the bottom of the Avenyn is **Kungsparken** with trees, shrubs and lawns beside the canal. To the right is the **Trädgårdsföreningens**, a marvellous garden with trees and shrubs, a rosarium (which draws rose lovers from across Europe), a palm house (with camellias, tropical plants and free-flying parrots), a butterfly house, and an excellent café (open 07:00–19:30 daily May–Aug; 09:00–16:00 daily Sep–Apr).

Cross the canal and continue along Östra Hamngatan. To the left, along Kungsgatan, is the **Domkyrkan** (cathedral) built in 1815 to replace one destroyed in one of the periodic fires which ravaged medieval Gothenburg. A little further on, in Södra Hamngatan to the left, is the **Residenset**, the mid-17th-century Governor's residence where King Karl X Gustav died. Beyond the next canal is **Gustav Adolfs Torg**, with the **statue** of the king at its centre. Bordering the square are the 17th-century **Rådhuset** and **Borsen** (stock exchange). Leave the square along Norra Hamngatan to reach the **Stadsmuseet**, the city museum housed in the old Swedish East India Company building. The museum explores the city's history and has a superb collection of East Indian porcelain (open 10:00–17:00 daily; closed Mon Sep–Apr).

North of the Stadsmuseet is the **Kronhuset**, the city's oldest secular building. It is now an exhibition/concert hall, while its courtyard houses small craft shops. North again is the **Maritime Centre**, one of the world's biggest, with 15 historical ships including a submarine (open 10:00–18:00 daily May–Aug; 10:00–16:00 daily Mar, Apr, Oct, Nov). At the centre's northern end is the new, and controversial, **Opera House**. Across the Lilla Bommens, the former entrance to the canal system, are *Barken Viking*, a 1906 training ship, now a hotel and restaurant, and the spectacular **Götheborgs-Utkiken**, an 86m (282ft) skyscraper. From the top there is a great view of the city.

Turning left along the canal from the Avenyn, the visitor can walk through Kungsparken to reach, to the left, the 19th-century **Hagakyrkan**. It stands close to **Haga**, the oldest part of the city, dating from the early 17th century. The district has now been renovated and is excellent for cafés, galleries and craft shops, or just for a stroll. Across the canal from Haga the **Feskekörka** in Rosenlundsgatan is a fish market built in 1874. The building, which because of its resemblance to a church is known locally as the Fish Church, has a good restaurant.

Above: *Utkiken and the* Barken Viking *in an attractive area of 'new' Gothenburg.*

From Järntorget, at the west end of Haga, head southwest, passing the impressive neo-Gothic **Oscar Fredriks Kyrka**, one of the city's most distinctive churches, to reach **Slottsskogsparken** – a fine, large park. Here there is an animal park, tropical house (reptiles and spiders), and children's zoo. South again, the city's **Botanical Gardens** are Sweden's largest with over 12,000 plant species.

Finally, head southeast from Götaplatsen to visit **Lisebergs**, Scandinavia's largest amusement park (basically open 11:00–23:00 or 15:00–23:00 daily May–Sep, but times vary). It has rides for everyone from the nervous to the macho, a vast tower offering great views, a Maxxima cinema, theatre, restaurants, cafés and more.

BOHUSLÄN
Inland Bohuslän *

North of Gothenburg, at **Kungälv**, the Bohus Fästning was built in the early 14th century by the Norwegians to protect what was then their border with Sweden. The picturesque ruins of the castle are well worth visiting if you are following the Göta älv north, or heading for the coast. Close to the castle, **Surte** has a good glassworks museum (open 11:00–16:00 daily May–Aug). It

---

THE BIRTH OF THE BALL BEARING

During the late 19th century, in one of Gothenburg's leading textile factories, Gamlestadens Fabrikers AB, a young engineer called Sven Wingqvist was wrestling with the problem of improving the reliability of the mechanical looms. Too often the looms seized and occasionally overheating that resulted threatened to burn the factory down. Wingqvist's solution was to invent spherical pieces of metal which allowed the machinery to run freely, reducing friction and the likelihood of seizure. He had invented the ball bearing. His managers saw the advantages of the system and soon the SKF company was formed to market the bearings. SKF is still a world leader in ball-bearing manufacture.

Above: *Smögen is claimed to be the most picturesque of all Bohuslän's fishing villages.*

KING TRYGGVE'S GRAVE

It is said that in early Viking times the herring were so numerous in the Kattegatt that it was possible to walk across the sea from Smögen to Hällo, the offshore island, on the shoals. The area was ruled by King Tryggve, but coveted by a powerful noble-woman who persuaded her sons to kill the king. He is said to lie beneath *Kung Tryggves Grav* on the island of Trysggö. Tryggve's pregnant wife, Astrid, escaped the murderers and, after many adventures, reached Norway where, years later, her son, Olav Tryggvason, became king.

was at the Surte glass-works that Alexander Samuelson designed the Coca-Cola bottle.

In the valley of the Göta älv there is a surprisingly fascinating museum of rope-making at **Älvängen**. To the north, at **Lödöse**, there is an equally inter-esting museum of the history of the valley be-fore Gothenburg existed.

Trollhättan is an industrial town, home of Saab and with a museum to the cars produced here (open 10:00–18:00 daily Jun to mid-Aug; 10:00–16:00 Tue–Fri mid-Aug to May). The local hydroelectric power station includes a visitor centre and, much more spectacular, the water that powers it is allowed to take its old route, down a long waterfall, at 15:00 daily.

Nearby, **Vänersborg**, at the southern tip of the vast Vänern, is famous for its forested plateau which forms a nature reserve in which elk roam. The Naturum illus-trates the wildlife of the reserve (open 11:00–20:00 daily), and safaris to view (with luck) the elk and other wildlife can be organized. The local museum also has an excellent (but curious – why here?) collection of Namibian and South African birds, as well as Swedish species, and other interesting items (open 12:00–16:00 Tue–Thu, Sat, Sun).

Coastal Bohuslän ★

On the coast there are a succession of attractive fishing villages backed by beautiful scenery. **Marstrand** has old buildings set around the 17th-century Carlstens fortress, while on **Tjörn**, the island to the north, **Åstol** is stunningly attractive. Nearby **Klädesholmen** has a museum to the herring trade which has sustained the local villages. Open 15:00–19:00 Sat and Sun Jun–Aug (daily in Jul). North again, on **Orust**, **Mollösund** is another picturesque village. On the mainland, west of Uddevalla, **Smögen** is claimed by many to be the most picturesque of all.

Uddevalla is a good centre for exploring the northern part of Götaland. The local museum covers folk history, particularly boat-building and fishing. Open 10:00–20:00 daily (until 16:00 Fri–Sun); closed Mon Sep–May.

More ancient history dominates at the Vitlycke Museum near **Tanumshede**. The local area has over 30,000 Bronze-Age rock engravings, the museum illustrating many of the best (open 10:00–18:00 daily Apr–Sep; 11:00–17:00 Thu–Sun Oct–Dec). The carvings are of hunts and ships, but also include explicitly sexual scenes.

To the north, at **Strömstad**, boat trips cross to the **Koster islands** (good beaches and a jazz festival in July) and search for seals.

DALSLAND *

East of Strömstad – visitors can take a short cut through Norway – is **Ed**, a centre for exploring the beautiful and wild Dalsland country. To the east, at **Håverud**, the aqueduct of the Dalsland Canal is an engineering masterpiece and also extremely picturesque. At nearby **Åsensbruk** the Dalsland Museum and Art Gallery is claimed to be the most beautiful in Sweden (open 10:00–18:00 Tue–Sun Apr–Dec). Slightly north of Håverud, at **Bengtsfors**, an extraordinary museum (Halmens Hus) is devoted to straw and its use in building and crafts (open 11:00–18:00 daily May–Sep; 12:00–16:00 Thu, Sat, Sun Mar, Apr, Oct, Nov).

> **THE BLOMSHOLM SHIP SETTING**
>
> At Blomsholm, near Strömstad, there is an Iron-Age cemetery and the second biggest ship setting in Sweden. Ship settings are upright stones set in the shape of a ship, with large prow and stern stones, which cover graves. It is assumed that the ship was to convey the spirits of the dead on their journey to the afterlife. The Blomsholm ship is over 40m (44yd) long and is made of 49 stones; the prow and stern stones are over 3m (10ft) high. Most experts date it to about AD500, the early Viking period, but it might be older. There is a legend that dead soldiers from a battle between Sweden and Norway in the early 18th century were also buried here.

Left: *The Bronze-Age rock carvings near Tanumshede are some of the best and most numerous in Europe.*

VÄSTERGÖTLAND **

East of Gothenburg is **Borås**, a town with a good shopping centre and a museum to its textile industry. Here too is a zoo which claims to be 'Sweden's First Africa' though it has Scandinavian species as well. The zoo is part of several conservation programmes including the European bison. Open daily 10:00–16:00 Jun to mid-Sep (until 18:00 in Aug), some weekends in winter.

East again is **Jönköping**, nicely positioned at the southern tip of Vättern. There is an infamous story of a young lady seduced by a man who claimed to be a Swedish wood and phosphorus executive, only to discover he sold matches on a street corner. Jönköping is to blame: the first match factory was started here in 1845 by the brothers Johan and Carl Lundström. The factory was not without its problems: the use of phosphorus in the striking head resulted in many workers suffering with 'phossy jaw', a facial gangrene caused by chemical fumes. Matches have long gone as a source of the town's prosperity, but it does have what it claims to be the world's only match museum (a claim rather spoilt by the recent opening of a tobacco and match museum in Stockholm!) which includes a collection of boxes and labels (10:00–17:00 daily Jun–Aug; 12:00–16:00 Tue–Fri, 11:00–15:00 Sat, Sun Oct–May).

The match museum is one of a phenomenal range of museums in the town, these including

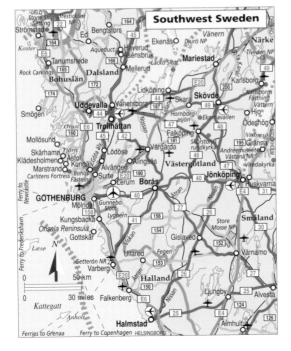

those to the local fire brigade, birds, photographs and radio. By far the most entertaining is the **Länsmuseum** (open 13:00–17:00 Tue–Sun) which includes not only local history but a collection of the work of the artist John Bauer. His ethereal fantasy works are enchanting. Children will love them, and may also find the town's Tropikhusset with its reptiles and monkeys a delight (open 10:00–17:00 daily).

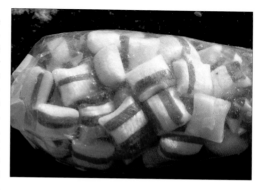

Above: *Gränna peppermint rock, made in the town but famous throughout Sweden.*

East of the town, but essentially a suburb of it, is **Huskvarna**, famous for the Husqvarna motorcycle, sewing machine and chainsaw factory. There is a museum to the products (open 10:00–17:00 Mon–Fri, 13:00–16:00 Sat, Sun Jun–Aug; 13:00–16:00 Sat, Sun Sep–May). Huskvarna also has a history museum, which includes underwater archaeological finds from Vättern, housed in an old gunpowder mill.

North of Huskvarna the **Västanå Nature Reserve** lies between the E4 motorway and Vättern. It was set up to protect an area of woodland and cliffs which is home to rare flowers, such as hepatica, and birds, including the scarlet grosbeak.

Nearby **Gränna** is famous for its Andréemuseet and its peppermint rock. In 1897 Salomon August Andrée attempted to become the first man to reach the North Pole. He took off from Svalbard with companions Nils Strindberg and Knut Frœnkel in an open basket beneath a hydrogen-filled balloon. The attempt was doomed from the start and the trio were never seen again. Then, in 1930, a Norwegian team landed on Kvitøya, a rarely visited Svalbard island, and found the remains of the men. Their flight had ended when ice on the balloon caused it to crash. They had struggled across the sea ice to Kvitøya, and there they had died. Remarkably the film in the team's camera had been preserved by the cold,

---

GIANT FOOTSTEPS

Set midway between Gränna and the western shore of Vättern is the island of Visingsö. Legend has it that a local giant called Vist wanted to cross the lake with his wife. She did not want to get wet, and he did not want to get his huge feet wet either. Rather than walk around the lake the lazy giant threw a piece of turf into the water. His stepping stone became Visingsö.

Above: *Andrée's stricken balloon on the ice after the crash. This photo was only discovered when the team's bodies were found.*

SHE LOST HER HEART

The last acts of the Andrée expedition were immensely moving. The bodies were brought home from Kvitøya by a ship accompanied, as it neared port, by a flotilla of smaller craft. There was a state funeral attended by the Swedish king. Most touching of all was the gesture by Gilbert Hawtrey, an English schoolmaster living in New Hampshire. Anna Charlier, Nils Strindberg's fiancée, had married Hawtrey when all hope of Nils's return was gone. She had accompanied Hawtrey to the US and taught piano at his school. She died before the discovery on Kvitøya. Hawtrey had Anna's body exhumed and her heart sent to Sweden to be buried beside her first love.

---

and developed photographs showed the last moments of the expedition. These poignant shots are on display in the museum (open 10:00–19:00 daily mid-Jun to Aug; 10:00–16:00 daily Sep to mid-Jun).

Gränna's peppermint rock – *polkagrisar* – is eaten throughout Sweden, but is primarily made here. The rock factories allow visitors to watch the process.

Southeast of Gränna lies Sweden's finest wooden medieval church. The **Viredakyrka** was built in the mid-14th century, but was extended (in stone) in the 16th century. Inside there are superb 15th-century frescoes.

Taking the E20 east from Gothenburg, visitors reach **Lerum**, close to which **Nääs Slott** is a fine example of a late 19th-century manor house, lavishly furnished in period style. At midsummer, the manor is the venue for a festival of Swedish traditional music and dance, while at Christmas there is a market (tours at 12:00, 13:00, 14:00, 15:00 daily mid-Jun to Aug; same times Sat, Sun, only May to mid-Jun, Sep).

Northeast, at **Alingsås**, there is a small zoo, chiefly showing Swedish animals. Nearby, steam trains still run in summer on a length of old track. There is also a railway museum. **Falköping** has an interesting local history museum but is mainly a base to head east to visit the **Skörstorps rundkyrka**, a rare 12th-century round church, or north to **Ekornavallen** where there is an impressive megalithic site (*see* page 14).

Skara has an interesting cathedral and a museum of Västergötland which includes 16 bronze shields placed in Vänern in about 1000BC and found only recently. The question of why these magnificent shields were sunk is one which has baffled experts ever since the discovery (open 10:00–17:00 Tue–Fri, 10:00–21:00 Wed, 12:00–17:00 Sat, Sun).

At nearby **Skövde** the museum has a replica of another outstanding local find: a horde of gold objects (open 12:00–18:00 Tue–Thu, 10:00–16:00 Fri, 10:00–13:00 Sat, 13:00–17:00 Sun).

Northwest of Skara, **Lidköping** is a lovely little town on a deep bay of Vänern. The area around Limtorget is very picturesque, with many 17th-century houses. The courthouse in Nya Stadens Torg looks almost as old, but is a 1960 replica of the original which was destroyed by fire.

Close to the town, **Stola Herrgård** is an early 18th-century manor house furnished in period style (open Apr–Sep by appointment only). Rather more imposing is **Läckö Slott** perched at the end of the peninsula that forms the Lidköping bay. Built in the 17th century in Baroque style, the castle replaced a medieval one. With over 200 rooms, the castle is a remarkable place for such a seemingly remote area (tours only: 10:15–16:30 daily May–Aug; 11:00–13:00 daily Sep).

Northeast of Lidköping, beyond Mariestad, the visitor reaches the Göta Canal. Follow this southeast to **Karlsborg** where the vast Karlsborgs Fästning is said to have been one of the largest building projects of its day. Unfortunately it took almost a century to complete, and by that time (1909) such fortresses were hopelessly out of date. The castle is worth a visit, perhaps to walk its 5km

DANCING CRANES

Between Skara and Skövde, and close to the megalithic site of Ekornavallen, is **Hornborgasjön**, a lake that is the centrepiece of a nature reserve famous throughout Sweden for its bird life. Though some come to see eagles and ospreys, most bird-watchers time their visit to see the spectacular dance of the 4000 pairs of common cranes that arrive in March to breed. The mating dance can be seen until the end of April.

THE GÖTA CANAL

The canal was constructed to link the North and Baltic seas, achieving this by linking a river and eight lakes with three sections of canal that require 65 locks. It took over 20 years to construct and involved 60,000 soldiers moving 300,000m^3 (392,400 cubic yards) of rock. The driving force behind this was Baltzar von Platen who sadly died in 1830, three years before the opening ceremony. Tourism on the canal began early: Thomas Cook used steamships to follow the canal in the 1870s. Today visitors can travel its length in style and comfort, exploring what has been called Sweden's linear national park. The journey from Gothenburg to Stockholm (or vice versa) takes 4 or 6 days depending on which ship is used.

Left: *The Göta Canal at Gothenburg.*

ÄSKHULT

There are a whole host of museums in the area around Kungsbacka, the best of which is the 18th-century village of Äskhult which is now the open-air museum of Fjärås Bräcke. Äskhult was only ever four farms, with fewer than 40 inhabitants at any one time, the population dwindling throughout the 20th century until the last villager died in 1964. The houses have never been painted, the glazed, weather-beaten wood adding an extra poignancy to the deserted village.

(3-mile) perimeter or to inspect its countless buildings, one of which is a military museum. Tours at 13:00 May–Aug (more tours in July).

Head south along the edge of Vättern, perhaps pausing to enjoy the quaint wooden town of **Hjo** or turning off at **Habo** to visit one of Sweden's best wooden churches.

HALLAND *

South of Gothenburg – leave the E6/E20 at Mölndal Öst and head for Manegen – is **Gunnebo Slott**, built in the late 18th century for one of Sweden's richest merchants. The dazzling white house, looking almost as if it were made of icing sugar, is exquisite, decorated and furnished in understated style. The beautiful surrounding parkland and gardens add to the serenity, and produce organic vegetables for the restaurant. The house is occasionally the venue for concerts (open 10:00–17:00 daily May–Sep; 11:00–16:00 Sun Oct–Apr). Nearby, **Råda Manor** is another fine 18th-century house, beautifully set beside a lake, that also has a fine restaurant.

To the south **Kungsbacka** is a neat town with a very pretty centre of late 19th- and early 20th-century houses. From it a delightful excursion crosses the Onsala Peninsula to the picturesque resort of **Gottskär**. South of Kungsbacka there are a number of excellent beaches, some sandy, some rocky. **Varberg** has been a popular bathing resort town since the 19th century and is now renowned for its nudist beaches. The town boasts a mighty 13th-century castle which houses two extraordinary items. Bocksten Man is a 600-year-old murder victim. The man was garrotted, then drowned and finally had three stakes thrust through him before being dumped in a local bog. The remarkable thing is that the bog preserved his clothing, Europe's only example of a complete medieval garb, with hood, cloak, stockings and shoes. That makes the body unique, but the eye is drawn not to the clothing, but to the thick red hair around the tiny skull – this was once a man. The other item is a small brass button, reputedly the bullet that shot King Karl XII in 1718. The King's wars were ruining Sweden, but his enemies were convinced that he had supernatural

powers and could only be killed by a personal item. They stole a button from his uniform, added lead and shot him in the head. The castle is open 10:00–18:00 daily mid-Jun to mid-Aug; 10:00–16:00 daily mid-Aug to mid-Jun. On a more cheerful note, close to Varberg the **Getterön Nature Reserve** is famous for its geese and wader populations.

Falkenberg, next along the coast, has a lovely old bridge beside which are the ruins of a medieval castle torn down by irate peasants in the early 15th century. The town also has a fine museum to the history of photography. **Halmstad**, the 'capital' of Halland, was Danish until 1645, its coat of arms (three crowned hearts) a gift from Danish King Christian IV for resisting a Swedish attack. King Christian also built the castle, beside which, in the Nissan River, the *Najaden* is the world's smallest full-rigger. The ship, built in 1897, is open to visitors. The town museum is excellent, but children will prefer the Tropikcenter with its reptiles, monkeys and birds. Open 10:00–18:00 daily May–Aug (until 20:00 in Aug); 10:00–16:00 daily Sep–Apr], and the Miniland model village with miniatures of Sweden's most famous buildings. These can be viewed, in part, from a narrow-gauge railway. Open 10:00–16:00 daily (until 18:00 Sun) May–Sep.

Above: *The* Najaden *at Halmstad – the world's smallest full-rigged ship.*

A Cautionary Tale

Close to Kungsbacka lies **Tjöholm Slott**, built in the 1890s by James Dickson, a wealthy Scottish merchant. Dickson was a horse lover – his vast stables are now a café, and a museum houses his carriages (and, uniquely, a horse-drawn vacuum cleaner). The house is open to visitors and is an interesting place. Sadly Dickson did not enjoy it for long. It is said that he cut his hand opening a bottle of champagne, used the lead cap as a temporary bandage, contracted blood poisoning and died.

Southwest Sweden at a Glance

BEST TIMES TO VISIT

Summer is best for the beaches south of Gothenburg and for most visitor sites. Spring is also excellent, particularly for bird-watchers. Autumn is pleasant if the North Sea's storms hold off. As elsewhere, winter is cold and can be bleak.

GETTING THERE

By air: There are direct flights to Gothenburg from many European cities, and internal flights to the city from Stockholm. A regular bus service runs from the airport to the city bus station (close to the railway station). The journey takes about 30 minutes. There are also airports at Halmstad, Jönköping and Skövde, and the airport at Malmö is only two hours or so from Gothenburg by car.
By train: From Gothenburg there are lines to Vänersborg and north along the shore of Vänern; north through Bohuslän to Fredrikstad (Norway), along the coast to Malmö, and inland to Skövde. Services are regular and punctual.
By road: The Öresund link makes it possible to reach Gothenburg easily from Copenhagen (and, therefore, the European motorway system). The E6 (starting as a motorway, but becoming a single carriageway) heads north from Gothenburg, through Bohuslän to the Norwegian border. The E20 (also starting from Gothenburg as a motorway

but becoming an 'ordinary' road) goes to Skara, Mariestad and Örebro. The E6/E20 is motorway all the way to Malmö. It hugs the coast, making journeys to Falkenberg and Halmstad fast and efficient.
By ferry: Gothenburg is linked by ferry to Oslo, Copenhagen, the UK (Harwich and Newcastle) and Germany (Kiel). There is a ferry to Frederikshavn in Denmark's Jutland. Varberg is linked by ferry to Grenaa (Jutland) in Denmark.

GETTING AROUND

The **train** service is very good, linking many towns and villages. The **roads** are also good and usually empty. **Buses** are reasonable, but limited (in terms of the numbers). Gothenburg has nine **tram** lines which all meet at Brunnsparken close to the main train station. Trams are the quickest way of travelling longer journeys in the city. One tramway takes visitors to the Liseberg amusement park.

WHERE TO STAY

Gothenburg has very good hotels (and a good range). Other main towns also offer good opportunities. The local Tourist Offices usually have lists and booking services.

LUXURY
Radisson SAS Scandinavia Hotel, Södra Hamngatan 59-65, 401 24 Göteborg, tel: 31 758 5000, fax: 31 758 5001.

This and the Elite Plaza are the best hotels in town. Very elegant with its central atrium (with a restaurant). Every possible facility; excellent service.
Elite Plaza Hotel Göteborg, Västra Hamngatan 3, Box 11065, 404 22 Göteborg, tel: 31 720 4000, fax: 31 720 4010. Another beautiful hotel with all conceivable services. Very good position.
Elite Stora Hotellet, Hotellplan, Box 23, 551 12 Jönköping, tel: 36 100 000, fax: 36 719 320. A Best Western Elite hotel. Well sited for the town and the local area. Very comfortable; excellent facilities.

MID-RANGE
Best Western Mornington Hotel Göteborg, Kungsportsavenyn 6, 411 36 Göteborg, tel: 31 767 3400, fax: 31 711 3439. One of the best positioned hotels in town, at the bottom of the main street. Straightforward and a little basic, but very comfortable. Close to excellent restaurants.
Rica City Hotel Göteborg, Burggrevegatan 25, 411 03 Göteborg, tel: 31 771 0080, fax: 31 771 0089. Rica City chain hotel; renowned for good position, comfort and quiet, unfussy efficiency.
First Hotel Mårtenson, Storgatan 52, 302 43 Halmstad, tel: 35 177 575, fax: 35 125 875. First chain hotel; upper end of the mid-range. Pleasant rooms; good service. Arguably the best position in town.

Southwest Sweden at a Glance

BUDGET

BUDGET

Hotel Flora, Grönsakstortorget 2, 411 17 Göteborg, tel: 31 138 616, fax: 31 132 408. Very pleasant; close to canal, Kungsparken and Haga, and not too far from all the other sites either. Excellent value.

Örgryte Hotel, Danska Vägen 68-70, 415 59 Göteborg, tel: 31 707 8900, fax: 31 707 8999. A 20–30 minute walk (or short bus ride) east of the main centre. Comfortable and well maintained.

Hotell Skövde, Stationsgatan 10, 541 30 Skövde, tel: 500 410 645, fax: 500 410 661. An inexpensive, unfussy, neat and tidy hotel from which to explore the area between the two big lakes. Well appointed and very friendly.

WHERE TO EAT

All the main towns have excellent restaurants, the coastal ones often specializing in seafood. **Gothenburg** has some of the best restaurants in Sweden (certainly the best outside Stockholm).

Fiskekrogen at Lilla Torget 1 (tel: 31 101 005) for fish, and **Steak** at Arkivgatan 7 (tel: 31 185 015) for meat.

Tvåkanten, Kungsportsavenyn 27, 411 35 Göteborg, tel: 31 182 115. Absolutely charming restaurant halfway along the main street. Excellent menu and faultless service.

Outside Gothenburg the list of possibilities is almost endless. Worth considering is: **Borgmästaren**, Borgmästargränd 19, 551 14 Jönköping, tel: 36 161 440. A delightful place at the centre of town. Huge menu; good wine list.

SHOPPING

In Gothenburg, **Nordstan** is the biggest shopping complex in Scandinavia with 150 shops as well as cafés and restaurants. Fredsgatan is another area of mixed shopping which includes an NK (Nordiska Kompaniet) department store. Kunsgatan has fashion and shoe shops and the streets that run from it – Vallgatan and Viktoriapassagen for example – also have fashion and design shops, and good cafés. Kungsportsavenyn has expensive shops, chiefly selling furnishings, and Bohusslöjds, a departmental store, is especially good for craft items. For souvenirs and gifts, try Haga where galleries and craft outlets have contributed to the regeneration of the area. There are daily markets in Kungstorget, while Kronhusboderna, the Kronhuset courtyard, has excellent craft shops. The main towns have small shopping centres and many towns and villages sell local art and crafts.

TOURS AND EXCURSIONS

Gothenburg offers a city pass (the Göteborg Pass) which gives free entry to most museums, free travel on city buses and trams, and discounts in some shops and restaurants. Gothenburg has sightseeing tours by bus, horse and carriage, and boat. Boat trips visit the archipelago to the north and the Elfborg fortress on a small island at the mouth of the Göta älv. Evening cruises around the coast and archipelago are popular. Most offer dinner and some have live music. The Tourist Information Offices have details of excursions. These are limited, but some tour companies do exist.

USEFUL CONTACTS

Tingshustorget, 666 21 Bengtsfors, tel: 531 526 354, fax: 531 10855.
Kungsportsplatsen 2, 411 10 Gothenburg, tel: 31 612 500, fax: 31 612 501.
Brahegatan 38, 563 22 Gränna, tel: 390 41010, fax: 390 10275.
Halmstads Slott, Box 47, 301 02 Halmstad, tel: 35 132 320, fax: 35 158 115.
Resecentrum, 551 89 Jönköping, tel: 36 105 050, fax: 36 107 768.
Na Hamnen, Box 98, 452 22 Strömstad, tel: 526 62330, fax: 526 62335.
St Oppen 5, 457 91 Tanumshede, tel: 525 20400, fax: 525 29860.
Järnvägsgatan, Box 147, 462 22 Vänersborg, tel: 521 271 400, fax: 521 271 401.
Göta Canal boats: AB Göta Kanalbolag, Box 3, 591 21 Motala, tel: 141 202 050, fax: 141 215 550.

7
Northern Sweden

Even a glance at the map of Sweden shows that on the basis of the distance from Malmö to Kiruna, to define the north of the country as starting at Uppland's northern border is open to ridicule as two-thirds of the country lies that way. But there are good reasons for doing so. Within Sweden the north is defined as the country beyond the Dalälven River, which runs south of Falun and Gävle. There is also a distinct change in the scenery, from wooded, but low-lying, to upland, mountainous.

This chapter considers the country from Uppland to the Arctic Circle. It is a land of interest and contrast. The **Falun** copper mine was once the world's most important producer. There are iron mines too, the steel works they supported being the basis of Sweden's industrialization. **Gysinge** and the towns around it were important steel-making centres. Nearby **Gävle** is home to Sweden's national railway museum and lies on one of the most attractive sections of the Swedish coast.

To the north are interesting towns, **Sundsvall** and **Östersund**, the latter set on the shores of the beautiful **Storsjön**, a lake with a monster to rival that of Loch Ness. To the west the increasingly mountainous country that leads to the Norwegian border is walking and skiing country. Here lies **Åre**, Sweden's premier ski resort.

North again are **Umeå**, **Skellefteå** and **Luleå**, all historically interesting and good centres for exploring the long valleys which cut through rugged country to reach Norway. The culture of these northern towns and vil-

Don't Miss

*** Falun: phenomenal remains of the one of the world's most important copper mines.
*** Glösäbacken: the beautiful and inspiring prehistoric carvings of elk.
** Åre: If you are skiing.
** Färnebofjärden National Park: for its birds.
* Östersund: the Överhogdal Tapestry of Viking life in the museum.
* Tännforsen: an awe-inspiring waterfall.

Opposite: *Copper has been mined at Falun since the 13th century.*

Above: *Looking down the huge, and terrifying, ski jump at Falun.*

FALUN COPPER MINE

It is likely that the Falun mine was worked in Viking times. Certainly it was productive in the 13th century and by the 17th century was the most important in the world. It closed in December 1992. Today it is open to visitors who can wonder at the Great Pit, caused by a collapse on 25 June 1687. As it was the Midsummer Festival the mine was closed and so no one was killed. The collapse is a central theme of the mine; 3D technology portrays the event which resulted in a 100m (328ft) deep and 400m (437yd) wide chasm. The museum has more information.

---

lages has been influenced by the proximity of Finland and also by the Sámi peoples who still live in the valleys.

DALARNA ***

Using the E18 and then road No. 70 from Stockholm, Dalarna is reached at **Avesta** where the old village is beautifully preserved. The smelting house of the old metalworks is now a coin museum. Close to the village is the world's largest Dala horse, the Trojan-like horse that is so popular a souvenir. This one stands 13m (43ft) high and weighs about 70 tons – rather too big for the average suitcase.

To the north, at **Hedemora**, the theatre in an old wooden barn is the oldest of its type in Sweden, a memory of an age when local folk made their own entertainment. Near the village the Hovran bird sanctuary has a tall observation tower, while to the northeast, at **Dala-Husby**, a collection of museums (called the Husby Ring) explores the ancient culture and industrial history of the area.

Säter is another well-preserved town, while **Borlänge**, a more modern town, has a museum devoted to a famous son, Jussi Björling, the operatic tenor (open 10:00–16:00 daily Jun–Sep).

Falun, the next town, is one of the highlights of the area; the Store Kopparberget mine and museum are an absolute must. Open 12:30–16:30 daily Jul–Aug (Sat, Sun only last two weeks of Aug. The town also has a famous sports centre (scene of Nordic Ski World Championships) with a 115m (377ft) ski jump. The town's Dalarna Museum is excellent and includes the library of Selma Lagerlöf, rescued when her Falun home was demolished (open 10:00–17:00 Mon–Fri, 12:00–17:00 Sat, Sun). At nearby **Sundborn**, the home of the artist Carl Larsson has been turned into a museum of his life and work (open 11:00–17:00 mid-June to mid-Aug, opens at 13:00 Sun).

Northwest of Falun, **Leksand** is the site of Sweden's most popular Midsummer Festival. The town church is 13th century and well worth a visit, as is the museum of the local area and the culture house with its folk costumes and art. South of the town, at **Gagnef**, there is a lace museum and the only log bridge now surviving in Sweden. North of Leksand, at **Siljansnäs**, is Sweden's largest exhibition centre on natural history, with an observation tower and marked trails. Children will also be thrilled by Adventure Summerland, an activities park close to Leksand.

Following road No. 70 around the Siljan Lake's northern edge is a marvellous trip. **Rättvik** is a summer sailing and winter skiing resort with a fine church and good local heritage centre. For children, the Sommar Rodel is a must: a wheeled toboggan run along a bobsleigh-like course. At **Nittsjö** the old ceramics factory is now a workshop for local ceramic artists, while **Mora**, at the northern end of the lake, is famous for the Vasaloppet ski race and as the home of the local artist Anders Zorn. There is a museum to Zorn which indicates the range of his work – landscapes, portraits, some almost surreal paintings, and fine sculptures. Open 12:00–17:00 daily (opens at 10:00 in summer). Close to Mora, at **Gesunda**,

THE VASALOPPET

In the 16th century Gustav Vasa tried to provoke an uprising against Danish rule but failed and retreated to Mora. His reception there was not enthusiastic and he set off to ski towards Norway. Soon after he had left, news of the Stockholm Bloodbath reached the town. Two skiers were dispatched to catch Gustav and return him to the town. The 90km (56-mile) Vasaloppet ski race from Sälen to Mora commemorates the return journey. Held annually in March, it attracts 15,000 competitors from 30 nations. The winning man takes about 4 hours, the leading lady about 30 minutes longer. In summer it is possible to hike the course. There is a museum to the event in the Vasaloppets Hus, Mora. Open 10:00–18:00 daily mid-May to Aug; 11:00–17:00 Mon–Fri Sep to mid-May).

Left: *Lake Siljan is the centrepiece of beautiful country.*

Santaworld (Father Christmas' 'official' home) is a summer activity park and, in winter, a place for elves, trolls and visitors (open 10:00–16:00 daily mid-Jun to mid-Aug; weekends only in winter). Also nearby, **Nusnäs** is where most Dala horses are made (at Nils Olsson Hemsløjd's studio – open 05:00–16:00 daily, closed Sun Sep to mid-June), while at **Grönklitt**, to the north, beyond Orsa, is Europe's largest park for free-roaming bears, wolves and lynxes.

Northwest of Orsa, **Älvdalen** has one of Sweden's most curious museums, to porphyry and accordions. Porphyry, an igneous rock in which crystals are set in a fine-grained rock mass, was quarried locally for use in decorative urns, etc. The accordions were made by the Hagströms company which also made guitars for such stars as Elvis Presley and The Beatles. Open 10:00–17:00 daily (closed Sat, Sun Oct–May). Northwest of the town visitors enter increasingly wild and beautiful country: west of **Särna**, which has a lovely wooden church, **Njupeskär** is Sweden's highest waterfall at 97m (318ft). Northwest of Särna, the **Töfsingdalen National Park** is famed for its plant life.

South of Särna, **Sälen** is a major ski resort as well as being the starting point for the famous Vasaloppet race. Further south, **Malung** has one of Sweden's best heritage museums arranged around 15th- and 16th-

century farmsteads. Continuing along road No. 71, then taking No. 247 from Björbo, brings the visitor to Ludvika at the southern end of the Väsman Lake. **Ludvika** is an industrial town with a mining history which is explored in the local museum. Some local mines are also open to visitors. Particularly good is Flogbergets, to the east. There is also a freshwater aquarium which shows all Sweden's species.

Above: *The old town of Gamla Gefle which lies to the south of new Gävle.*

GÄSTRIKLAND **

Gästrikland, one of Sweden's smallest regions and one with beautiful scenery, lies north of Uppland. Heading north you'll reach the region's first town, the old iron-working centre of **Gysinge** – the first place in the world to produce steel using electricity in 1900. North again is **Gävle**, most notable for the delicious smell of Gavilia coffee that hangs over it. The town has a famous railway museum (the National Museum) with one of the world's best collections of locomotives and carriages. Open 10:00–16:00 daily (closed Mon Sep–May). There are also museums to the forestry industry and to the life and poetry of Joe Hill, the US union man framed and executed for murder in Utah in 1915. Hill was born in Gävle. Close to the town there is a small zoo and leisure park at **Furuvik**, a coastal village.

North of Gävle the coast is known locally as the *Jungfrukusten*, the Virgin Coast. It has some lovely little fishing villages – **Utvalnäs** and **Bönan** are particularly attractive. West of Gävle there are reminders of the old iron industry at **Forsbaska** and **Högbo**. Högbo was the birthplace of the Sandvik AB steelworks. South of Sandviken, at **Årsunda**, there is a fine Viking museum

> ### THE FÄRNEBOFJÄRDEN NATIONAL PARK
>
> Close to Gysinge, the Färnebofjärden park was set up to protect the bird life of an area dominated by the Dalälven River. Ospreys and white-tailed sea eagles are the most sought-after species for bird-watchers, but other worthwhile sightings would be capercaillie, particularly a cockbird displaying from a prominent rock, and white-backed and black woodpeckers. In all, seven of Europe's eight woodpecker species can be found in the park.

and reconstructed village (open 10:00–16:00 daily May–Sep). From Sandviken, road No. 272 reaches **Ockelbo** where the churchyard has one of Sweden's finest rune stones, portraying the legend of Sigurd killing the dragon. West of the town, railway enthusiasts who loved the Gävle museum will want to visit **Talläs** and **Jädraås** which are linked by steam trains travelling a narrow-gauge railway.

SUNDSVALL AND ÖSTERSUND ★★★

North of Dalarna and Gästrikland lie a number of regions centred around the towns of Sundsvall and Östersund. Heading north to Sundsvall takes the visitor through **Hälsingland**, a wild and beautiful region. The area's animals can be seen at the zoo at **Jarvsö**, while on the coast **Skärså** is one of the most picturesque of all Swedish fishing villages. **Sundsvall** is a monument to 1880s architecture, having been rebuilt after a spark from a steamboat started a fire that burned down the wooden town. To the north, the **Höga Kusten** (High Coast) near Härnösand is generally considered the most attractive section of Sweden's coast.

Inland of Sundsvall, **Östersund** is a lovely place with an impressive town hall. The town museum houses the Överhogdal Tapestry, dated to about 1100 and showing late Viking life. It is probably the oldest tapestry in Europe. Open 11:00–17:00 daily (closed Mon mid-Aug to mid-June). Close to the town, at **Glösäbacken**, are the best Stone-Age rock carvings in Sweden: a herd of 45 elk heading uphill across dozens of rocks, a strangely inspiring sight.

Östersund is a good place from which to explore the ruggedly beautiful country which lies close to the border with Norway. The valley west of **Hede** is superb and has, at **Funäsdalen**, one of Sweden's newest museums. Opened by King Carl Gustav in 1999, it explores the culture of farmers, miners and Sámi people who made a living 'on the roof of Sweden'. Open 09:00–18:00 daily (open 11:00 Sat, Sun; closed Sat, Sun Oct–May). More famous is the valley west of Östersund, particu-

---

THE STORSJÖN MONSTER

Although less famous than Scotland's Loch Ness Monster, the one that inhabits Storsjön Lake is just as real to local inhabitants. Variously reported as being snake-like, with humps; between 3m and 14m long; to eat anything from fish to potatoes (it was once seen raiding a potato field at the lake edge); as grey or black in colour; and making a hissing or whining noise, the monster is said to have been created by local witches in medieval times. Your best chance of spotting the elusive creature is to wait for a day when the lake is mirror-smooth.

larly **Åre**, Sweden's best-known ski resort, one which can positively guarantee snow. Near Åre is **Tännforsen**, Sweden's most powerful waterfall, over 700m³ (150,000 gallons) of water falling 38m (125ft) per second.

NORTH TO THE ARCTIC

To the north of Sundsvall, **Örnsköldsvik** is a paper-making town – visitors can attempt to make paper by hand at the Kulturfabriken, or watch experts do it (usually rather better). Further north, **Umeå** is a university town famous for its birch trees. The town's Gammlia has several good museums, one exploring history from Sámi times. Inland, at **Vännäs**, there is a museum of old cars, motorcycles and fire engines, and the chance to take Europe's only jet boat for a ride up the Vindel River.

At **Vindeln**, to the north, the river is also the venue for the more adventurous who can follow it by raft. North of the town the rapids on the river are among the most impressive in Sweden, particularly those of the Mårdseleforsarna Nature Reserve.

To the west, at **Bjurholm**, the Älgens hus offers visitors the chance to get close to elk – even to touch them. For those who like their wildlife to be wild, a walk in the Balberget Nature Reserve offers the chance to see the animals. The reserve was set up to protect a unique flora which includes the northernmost occurrence of hazel.

HOLMÖN

From Norrfjärden, 35km (22 miles) north of Umeå, ferries cross to Holmön (taking about 40 minutes, the ferry is free), a 15km (9-mile) long island which holds the record for sunniest place in Sweden. The island can be explored by bicycle and for a holiday tale to surpass most others, visitors can spend the night in the lighthouse, now a hostel. Each July there is a rowing boat race from the island to Finland which is just 40km (25 miles) away.

CLIMATE

Sweden's climate starts to get serious now. **Summer** is still delightful: cool perhaps, but with long days that make warm, sunny weather seem as endless as the days of childhood. **Autumn**, however, comes sooner and has an edge to it. **Spring** is later, but for many is the finest time of all, epecially in the mountains when the flowers bloom. **Winter** is long, dark and cold.

Left: *Östersund is one of the prettiest towns to visit for those travelling north towards the Arctic.*

LULEÅ GAMMELSTAD

Luleå became important in medieval times when Sweden was in conflict with Russia over the border between the two countries, and it was in Stockholm's interest that a strong local lord arose with a power base in a coastal town. By the 14th century the town was the capital of a region that covered much of what is now northern Sweden, the old town growing as a church village, a collection of wooden houses that were occupied by the region's folk who had trekked in to attend the Sunday service but could not then, in winter, get home by nightfall. The church is the largest and finest in the north. The church village is worth exploring; a trail visits the best sites.

Below: *A street in Luleå Gammelstad. The old town was once the capital of northern Sweden.*

Skellefteå was once Sweden's gold-mining capital: at nearby **Boliden**, the gold-mine museum deals with the area's geology and mining history. In Skellefteå itself, be sure to visit the Lejanströms Bridge, Sweden's oldest and longest wooden bridge, built in 1737, and Bonnstan, a perfectly preserved village of 17th-century wooden houses. Beside it is the Nordanå park with a cultural museum and a playground for children. Children will also love Camp Caribo at nearby **Hemmistjörn**, with its climbing wall, aerial walkway and horse riding, and a trip on the world's longest cableway at **Örträsk**. The cableway is 13km (8 miles) long and formerly transported iron ore. Today the cars each carry four people on a two-hour trip above marshland and forest.

North of Skellefteå is **Piteå**, the area's main beach resort, and **Luleå**, the capital of northern Sweden. The obvious visitor site in the town is Gammelstad, but the 1890s cathedral and city art museum are also worth seeing.

Inland of these coastal towns is a vast mountainous wilderness, a country to delight the connoisseur of wild beauty. The church at **Dorotea** is decorated with sculptures by Carl Milles. From Dorotea, a beautiful road heads northwest to finish at **Borgafjäll**. At **Lycksele** there is a zoo of Nordic fauna, and a road to **Storuman** where a 7m (23ft) statue depicts the legendary wild man of the mountains. Much further along the same road, **Tärnaby** is a centre for exciting mountain excursions.

Road No. 95 runs inland to Arvidsjaur, then westward to **Sorsele**, famous for its fishing. On the road from Sorsele to **Ammarnäs**, a skiing and walking centre (and site of Sweden's most northerly potato field), **Brudslöjen** is one of the country's most beautiful waterfalls.

Northern Sweden at a Glance

BEST TIMES TO VISIT

Northern Sweden, south of the Arctic Circle, is an all-year area. In spring and summer the mountains are wonderful – long days, beautiful flowers. In autumn and winter they have guaranteed snow. The coast is at its best in summer, while spring and autumn add their own colours to a very picturesque area. Winter is cold with short days. Be prepared.

GETTING THERE

By air: There are airports at Arvidsjaur, Luleå, Lycksele, Sundsvall, Skellefteå and Umeå. They all have regular flights. Skyways also fly to/from Stockholm to airports at some of the smaller towns.
By train: There are a couple of railway lines; trains offer a fantastic way of seeing the country, particularly the Inlandsban (Östersund to Arvidsjaur).
By road: Plan for a long trip. There are express buses from Stockholm to Östersund and Umeå, which link with local services. It is a long drive from Stockholm to the Arctic Circle and the E4 is a single-carriage motorway. Stunning scenery.

GETTING AROUND

If travelling by bus and intending to get to the more remote places in the mountains you may find services are limited to one bus daily, or are even less frequent. The roads are, however, good and drivers will have few problems (if the snow

has cleared). Give yourself extra time as you will want to stop to take in the scenery, and your average speed will be low.

WHERE TO STAY

There are excellent hotels in all the main towns. The ski resorts have a range of accommodation. Book early for winter trips; summer is usually quieter.

LUXURY
Elite Stadshotellet Luleå, Storgatan 15, Box 924, 971 28 Luleå, tel: 920 67000, fax: 920 60787. One of the best hotels in the north. Well positioned; extremely comfortable.
Hotell Baltic, Sjögatan 11, 852 34 Sundsvall, tel: 60 150 720, fax: 60 123 456. Good service and facilities.

MID-RANGE
Scandic Hotel Skellefteå, Kanalgatan 75, 931 78 Skellefteå, tel: 910 752 400, fax: 910 752 411. Large and modern, but still intimate; good service.
Laisalidens Fjällhotell, 920 64 Tärnaby, tel: 954 21100, fax: 954 21163. The best alternative to a tent for those exploring the Kungsleden. Superb hotel; excellent service; help visitors get about. Wholesome meals if eating here.

BUDGET
Hotel Zäta, Prästgatan 32, 831 31 Östersund, tel: 63 517 860, fax: 63 107 782. Inexpensive, but very pleasant; good for exploring Härjedalen.

WHERE TO EAT

The main towns and villages have excellent restaurants. In the mountains the meals will usually be fairly basic, but the helpings will be large. Reindeer is likely to be on the menu.

SHOPPING

Not a great shopping area. Main towns have shopping centres and craft and gift shops, but more limited than towns to the south. The farther north you travel, the more Sámi crafts will be on offer.

TOURS AND EXCURSIONS

Tourist Information Offices and local hotels have details of the many tour operators.

USEFUL CONTACTS

Tourist Information Offices:
Dalgatan 47, 796 31 Älvdalen, tel: 251 80290/80294. Trotzgatan 10-12, 791 83 Falun, tel: 23 83050. Drottninggatan 37, 801 05 Gävle, tel: 26 147 430. Railway Station, Box 52, 793 22 Leksand, tel: 247 80300. Fredsgatan 10, 771 82 Ludvika, tel: 240 86050. Storgatan 43B, 971 31 Luleå, tel: 920 293 500/293 505. Stationsvägen, 792 32 Mora, tel: 250 26550. Storgatan 17, 795 22 Rättvik, tel: 248 797 210. Torget, 852 36 Sundsvall, tel: 60 610 450. Renmarkstorget 15, 903 26 Umeå, tel: 90 161 616. Torget, 830 13 Åre, tel: 647 1772. Rådhusgatan 44, 831 33 Östersund, tel: 63 144 001.

8
Lappland

Though Lappland is still used to describe that part of Sweden which lies north of the Arctic Circle, the now preferred name for the native people of the area is Sámi rather than Lapps. The Sámi are an ancient people, descendants of the Arctic coastal folk separated from their Asiatic steppe cousins by the growth of the taiga. At first the Sámi were a hunting and fishing people, but some time in the post-Viking era, perhaps as recently as 600 years ago, they domesticated reindeer. The early Sámi were probably nomadic, so the migratory habits of the reindeer would not have been a hardship. Today there are only domesticated reindeer in Scandinavia.

This tour of Lappland starts below the Arctic Circle, visiting **Arvidsjaur**, **Arjeplog** and **Vuollerim**, each with Sámi connections. North of the Circle is **Jokkmokk**, arguably Sweden's Sámi centre, and the twin centres of **Gällivare** and **Malmberget**. To the north is **Kiruna**, a town which has grown up around a huge ore mine. Near the town the **Ice Hotel**, surely the world's most extraordinary hotel, is built each year. In winter 2002–03 an **Ice Globe Theatre** was also built, a replica of Shakespeare's Globe in London, but in ice. Plays were staged in the Sámi language and, it is hoped, the theatre will become an annual event.

Finally we explore the **Arctic national parks**. It is here that the visitor is most likely to encounter the one flaw in the Arctic paradise – the mosquito. From late June to late August they appear in clouds. Though not dangerous, they are voracious and insistent, causing a great deal of irritation both with their presence and their bite.

DON'T MISS

*** Sarek National Park: one of the best parks in Europe. Fabulous scenery, but difficult to reach.
*** Kiruna: explore the iron mine.
** Arjeplog: the fascinating silver museum.
* Lappstaden: excellent Sámi cultural centre.

Opposite: *The interior of the Sámi church at Saltaluokta in the Padjelanta National Park.*

Above: Approaching the Treiksröset. The photographer is in Finland, the skier is in Sweden, while the mountains are in Norway.

CLIMATE

In **summer** the European Arctic is surprisingly benign. If the long days are sunny, they will also be warm and the mountains are beautiful (but swarming with mosquitoes). **Spring** and **autumn** are also beautiful, but **winter** is harsh and cruel. Be prepared.

TREIKSRÖSET

At the northern tip of Sweden is **Treiksröset**, the three country stone where Norway, Finland and Sweden meet. It is not reached by road on the Swedish side, the closest approach to it being from Kilpisjärvi in Finland. From there, a walk of 11km (7 miles), or a boat ride across a lake and a walk of about 3km (2 miles) reaches the stone.

CLOSE TO THE CIRCLE
Arvidsjaur *

Arvidsjaur was anciently the place where the Sámi used to meet for trade and debate, a fact which encouraged missionaries from the south, the first church being built here in 1606. Later, when silver was discovered locally, the town became an important supply point for prospectors, and the assay and shipment centre. The church village of about 80 tents and cabins has survived: one of the largest Sámi versions. The nomadic Sámi lived in teepees (called *lavvu* or *kåta*) made of reindeer hides draped over a birch pole framework, the basis of the church village. Called **Lappstaden**, the village is a centre for Sámi culture. Visits to reindeer breeding sites are possible and with luck visitors will hear the traditional Sámi *yoik*, a rhythmic song which is both oral tradition and entertainment.

Arjeplog and Vuollerim **

From Arvidsjaur, a worthwhile excursion visits **Arjeplog**, a town famous for its silver museum, founded by a local doctor, Einer Wallquist. The collection of Sámi silver here is probably the finest anywhere.

Finally, south of the Circle, at **Vuollerim** excavations are still in progress to prise the secrets of a Stone-Age society from the earth. The results of the excavations can be seen at the site museum.

ABOVE THE CIRCLE
Jokkmokk *

Jokkmokk (meaning 'bend in the river') has been the site of an important Sámi winter festival for over 400 years, its importance to the community encouraging missionaries to build a church in 1607. A winter festival is still held (from the first Thursday in February until the Sunday three days later) and is the best place for Sámi handicrafts. The festival includes reindeer racing – not for the faint-hearted (competitor or spectator). The town's **Ajtte Museum** is excellent for Sámi culture, with costume and silverware, and also has a garden of Swedish Arctic flora. Also worthwhile are the octagonal Lappkyrka (1870s replacement for the 18th-century original which was destroyed by fire) and the older wooden one.

Gällivare *

North of Jokkmokk is **Gällivare** (from the Sámi *djell vare*, 'a gap in the mountains'), much less attractive than Jokkmokk, but worth a visit for its Sámi church. South of the town the **Muddus National Park** is an untouched wilderness of pine forest and marshland where otter, elk, bear and wolverine roam.

Malmberget *

Almost twinned with Gällivare is **Malmberget** where the open-cast copper mine is Europe's biggest. The only attractive site is Kåkstan, a reconstruction of the original, 19th-century, mining settlement.

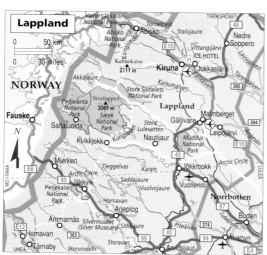

MIDNIGHT SUN AND AURORA BOREALIS

Because of the tilt of the earth's axis relative to the imaginary line linking the earth and the sun, the hours of sunlight vary through the year everywhere except at the Equator. The Arctic Circle (at about 66½°N) is the southern-most point at which the sun does not set on mid-summer's day, or rise on mid-winter's day. North of the circle in summer the 'midnight sun' shines, the length of time it can be seen increasing the further north you travel. At the North Pole there are 6 months of daylight and 6 months of night. At Kiruna (for example) the midnight sun can be seen from 29 May to 12 July. Because of the refraction of light the mid-night sun can occasionally be seen below the Arctic Circle: Arvidsjaur is the furthest south area where this occurs in Sweden.

As a compensation for the lack of winter sun above the Circle you may see the aurora borealis (you can see it in summer too if the night is dark enough). These beautiful shimmering lights, usually green but sometimes red, are the result of interactions between charged particles from the sun and air atoms high in the atmosphere.

The aurora are more often seen in high latitudes because of the strength of the earth's magnetic field as the pole is approached.

**KUNGSLEDEN –
THE KING'S WAY**

Kungsleden is one of the finest long-distance footpaths in Europe, stretching for about 350km (220 miles) from **Abisko** to **Hemavan**, a little way north of Tärnaby, a considerable fraction of the route therefore lying north of the Arctic Circle. The route crosses genuine wilderness and can even include an ascent of **Kebnekaise**, Sweden's highest peak. Yet despite its remoteness it is well signed, though accommodation (other than the backpacked tent) is scarce. Fit and experienced walkers should have no problems, and even casual walkers can enjoy a day or two on the route. To cross occasional marshland sections the route uses *spongs* (boardwalks), lemmings being startled out from beneath the timbers as the walker approaches.

Below: *There are no longer any wild reindeer in Scandinavia, the Sámi having domesticated them.*

Kiruna ***

Kiruna (Sámi *giron* – ptarmigan) is Sweden's most northerly town, an iron-mining town since 1899 and one which was of dramatic importance during World War II when its ore was coveted by Allies and Axis alike. Visitors can take a trip (summer only) down the deep (540m; 1800ft) iron-mine – a fascinating experience. The town is dominated by its town hall (Sweden's Most Beautiful Public Building of 1964) and has a beautiful church shaped like a traditional Sámi tent. There are also two excellent museums, the **Samegården** with its displays of Sámi culture and **Hjalmar Lundbohmsgården**, the home of the mine opener/city founder, which explores Kiruna's history.

The National Parks

At Sweden's western edge, adjoining the border with Norway, are a series of wonderful national parks. The most northerly, and also the smallest, is the **Abisko**, close to the town of the same name, a valley park with a varied flora. It is here that the Kungsleden trail starts.

South of the Abisko National Park is **Kebnekaise**, at 2111m (6926ft) Sweden's highest mountain. The first known ascent of the peak was in 1883 when the Frenchman Charles Rabot (wearing only underpants to protect 'my one and only pair of trousers') reached the top with two Norwegians, though it is likely that the Sámi had already climbed the peak.

South of Kebnekaise the **Stora Sjöfallets National Park** is home to rough-legged buzzards, grouse and ptarmigan, and vast areas of pine forest. To the southwest it links with the **Padjelanta National Park**, Europe's biggest national park at almost 2000km² (almost 800 square miles). Here there are gyrfalcons, golden eagles and snowy owls.

To the east is the **Sarek National Park**, the most remote and the most rugged, with dozens of glaciers and several peaks of over 2000m (6560ft). Here bears, wolverine and lynx roam in a landscape that is, perhaps, the finest and most beautiful in Europe.

Lappland at a Glance

BEST TIMES TO VISIT

Visit the mountains in late spring (when most snow has gone and flowers are blooming), in summer, or early autumn (when the cloudberries are ripe). In winter you can ski – cross country rather than downhill as there are few opportunities for the latter – or ride a snowmobile.

GETTING THERE

By air: There are airports at Arvidsjaur, Gällivare and Kiruna.
By rail: There are railway lines to Kiruna, through Jokkmokk and Gällivare, a truly awe-inspiring journey.
By road: The roads are reasonable, once the snow has melted, or with chains/studs for the more adventurous.

GETTING AROUND

Not as bad as it might at first appear, though the bus services are limited (both in season and in frequency).

WHERE TO STAY

There are good hotels in all the main towns.

LUXURY
Ice Hotel, 981 91 Jukkasjärvi (close to Kiruna), tel: 980 66 800, fax: 980 66890. One of the Arctic's strangest, yet most romantic, hotels. Each winter 30,000 tons of ice are used to create the Ice Hotel with 60 or so rooms, and bungalows with skylights for viewing the aurora. You are driven from Kiruna airport by snowmobile, sleep in sleeping bags on reindeer hides, and eat in an ice restaurant which serves great food. In spring, the hotel melts away and a new one is built the following winter.

Scandic Hotel Ferrum, Lars Janssonsgatan 15, 981 31 Kiruna, tel: 980 398 600, fax: 398 611. Built for businessmen, so unfussy and efficient.

MID-RANGE
Hotell Vinterpalatset, Järnvägsgatan 18, Box 18, 981 21 Kiruna, tel: 980 67770, fax: 980 13050. Close to the station. Converted 20th-century house. Log fire; excellent food.

Hotel Jokkmokk, Solgatan 45, 962 31 Jokkmokk, tel: 971 77700, fax: 971 77790. One of the best hotels in town. Beautiful views from most of the well-appointed rooms. Very comfortable.

Laponia Hotel, Storgatan 45, 933 33 Arvidsjaur, tel: 960 55500, fax: 960 55599. One of the best hotels in town and with the best restaurant. Good facilities (even an indoor pool).

BUDGET
There aren't many budget hotels here. If you have forgotten your tent, consider: **Gullriset Lägenhetshotell**, Bromsgatan 12, 981 36 Kiruna, tel: 980 10937, fax: 980 14700.

WHERE TO EAT

Can be a bit limited, but the better hotels all have excellent restaurants.

SHOPPING

Not a great shopping area, though most visitors are looking for Sámi crafts rather than fashion items. Sámi rituals form the basis of some craft items, but the Sámi were also skilled at embroidery and craft work. Their fabrics and silver, wood and horn work are favourite souvenirs. Good outlets are **Jokkmoks Tenn** in Jokkmokk, and **Mattarahkka** north of Kiruna.

TOURS AND EXCURSIONS

Available in vast numbers. At Kiruna there is gold-panning, horse riding, rafting, survival training and fishing. The Tourist Office has full details. There are similar opportunities in Jokkmokk and Gällivare.

USEFUL CONTACTS

Tourist Information Offices:
Torget, Box 4, 930 90 Arjeplog, tel: 961 14270, fax: 961 14279.
Garveregatan 4, 933 32 Arvidsjaur, tel: 960 17500, fax: 960 13687.
Storgatan 16, Box 56, 982 21 Gällivare, tel: 970 16660, fax: 970 14781.
Stortorget 4, Box 124, 962 23 Jokkmokk, tel: 971 12140/17257, fax: 971 17289.
Folkets Hus, Box 113, 981 22 Kiruna, tel: 980 18880, fax: 980 18286.

Travel Tips

Tourist Information

Sweden has Tourist Offices in all European capitals, North America, Australia, South Africa and Japan and in all main towns and most large villages throughout the country. Most offices help with accommodation and travel.

Entry Requirements

In general a valid passport is required by all travellers. For visitors from European Union (EU) countries a national identity card will suffice for visits of up to three months. Visitors from most European countries, North America, Australia and New Zealand do not require visas. Visitors from Colombia and many Asian, African and some ex-Soviet bloc countries do require a visa. If in doubt, ask at your Swedish Tourist Board office.

Customs

Visitors from countries outside the EU are restricted to one litre of spirits or two litres of fortified or sparking wine, together with two litres of table wine, and 200 cigar-ettes. Visitors from EU countries will know that 'duty-free' items are no longer available when travelling between Union countries. The following may be brought into the country, duty-paid from another EU country: 1.5 litres of spirits or 20 litres of spark-ling wine or 90 litres of table wine, 15 litres of strong beer and 300 cigarettes or 400g of tobacco.

Health Requirements

Sweden has no specific health requirements for visitors. Visitors from EU countries should carry an E111 form and present it when seeking treatment. Be aware that there are advantages in also having travel insurance (for instance in getting home quickly and, if necessary, with medical assistance). Visitors from other countries should check the validity and cover of their medical insurance. There is no easily negotiable general practitioner service in Sweden so if you are ill or have an accident it is best to present yourself at a local hospital. For emergency service tel: 112.

Getting to Sweden

By air: Sweden is 'co-owner' of SAS (Scandinavian Airlines) together with Denmark and Norway, and SAS is the major carrier into the country. Other European and world airlines also operate flights to Stock-holm. Many also operate flights to Malmö and Gothen-burg. Some European budget airlines also operate flights to Sweden – some land at Skav-sta, Stockholm's third airport; while some also use Malmö.

By sea: Sweden is linked by ferry with Denmark, Estonia, Finland, Germany, Lithuania, Norway, Poland and the UK. Most ferries carry cars – useful

---

ROAD SIGNS

Använd Helljus
• Use Headlights
Enkelriktad Gata
• One-Way Street
Gågata • Pedestrian Zone
Parkering Förbjuden
• No Parking
Parkeringplats • Car Park
Skola • School
Vägen Stängd • Road Closed
Omkörning Förbjuden
• No Overtaking

for visitors who wish to avoid a long drive. Several ferries link Sweden with Denmark, ships arriving in Gothenburg (from Frederikshavn), Varberg (from Grenaa), Helsingborg from Helsingør, Malmö (despite the Öresund bridge having apparently made the ship redundant), and also Ystad from Rønne on Bornholm. There are numerous carriers on these lines. Stockholm is linked to Tallinn in Estonia by the EstLine ships. The Finnish ferries are run by Silja Line and Viking Line. Scandline and TT-Line run the ships from Germany (mostly landing at Trelleborg, but there are ships to Gothenburg). Licso Line links Klaipeda in Lithuania with Stockholm. DFDS and Color Line run the ferries from Norway, DFDS also running those from the UK (Newcastle-Gothenburg: the Harwich-Esbjerg service can also be used as Esbjerg is only three hours drive from Copenhagen and the Öresund bridge). The Polish services are operated by Polferries, Unity Line and Stena Line.

By train: Sweden is connected by rail to all major cities in Europe, and beyond via the new Öresund link which has created a direct connection between Copenhagen and Malmö. Visitors arriving at Copenhagen's Kastrup airport will find that the high-speed train link with the city is actually a train from (and to) Malmö.

By road: There are direct road links with Norway and Finland. As with the trains, the new Öresund bridge has

opened a new option for road travellers. It is now possible to have breakfast in Copenhagen and dinner in Stockholm, after a long, but enjoyable, drive (perhaps with lunch at Kalmar).

What to Pack

Unless you are travelling to the north of the country in winter there is nothing particularly hostile about the Swedish climate. In summer a raincoat/ jacket is essential as you are likely to see rain. The sky is likely to be overcast at times, so bring something warm. Sweden is highly civilized and will have everything on sale, so there is no need to bring unnecessary items (though the cost of living is high, so such items as film – which you will need a lot of as there are great things to photograph – will probably be more expensive). In winter the situation is different, particularly if you are heading north. Sweden can be very, very cold and if a stiff wind is blowing the apparent temperature can plummet. Take plenty of warm and windproof clothing. Layered clothing is the best option.

Money Matters

Sweden has not, as yet, joined the Eurozone and so maintains its own currency, the **krona** (crown – the plural is **kronor**). The krona is divided into 100 öre, but there are only coins for 50 öre. There are 1, 5 and 20 kronor coins and 20, 50, 100, 500 and 1000 kronor notes. The krona is a convertible currency and so can be

HOLIDAYS AND FESTIVALS

Sweden has a whole host of festivals throughout the year, some international (music, arts, film, etc.), some more local, perhaps based on a local legend. It is worth finding out if there is anything coming up from the local Tourist Office as Swedes know how to have a good time. The following are Swedish public holidays:

New Year's Day
(Nyårsdag) 1 January
Epiphany
(Trettondedag Jul) 6 January
Good Friday (Långfredag)
Easter Monday
(Annandag påsk)
Labour Day
(Första Maj) 1 May
Ascension Day
(Kristi Himmelfärds dag)
Whit Monday
(Annandag Pingst)
Midsummer's Day
(Midsommardag)
first Friday after 21 June
All Saints' Day (Alla Helgons dag) 1 November
Christmas (Jul)
25 and 26 December

purchased abroad. Most Swedish banks have ATMs for credit and bank cards. Travellers cheques can be readily exchanged at all banks.

Accommodation

Sweden has a large number of excellent hotels, all towns and most large villages having something to offer the visitor. Several chains – Radisson SAS, Best Western, First, Rica City, Scandic, etc. – have numerous hotels throughout the country. These tend to be at the higher end of the price range, but budget hotels and youth hostels are available. There are many guest houses and bed-and-breakfast options which are inexpensive and allow travellers to meet Swedish people. There are many camp sites, chiefly around the coast. In the north, camping is supplemented by cabins, though these fill quickly, particularly in winter.

Eating Out

Eating out is one of the joys of a visit to Sweden as the menu will be packed with wholesome meals. Fish is a speciality, not only at coastal towns; some visitors coming across herrings for the first time at breakfast need a little time to adjust. Baltic salmon is another speciality. Elk and reindeer will be additions to the usual meats, particularly in the north. The larger towns offer not only Swedish cuisine, but also Chinese, Indian, Japanese and other menus. All restaurants and cafés serve tea and coffee, and most also serve hot chocolate. The latter is usually extremely good, and especially warming on cold winter days. Alcoholic drinks

are available in restaurants – the Danish Carlsberg and Tuborg beers and lagers, and imported wines – but they are not cheap. The Swedes do not have the same relaxed attitude to alcohol as the Danes. As with Norway, alcohol is only sold in state-controlled outlets and you will not be able to buy alcohol with a credit card as Swedes do not allow people to drink on credit.

Tipping

Service is usually included on restaurant and hotel bills, and even taxi fares, so check first. The 'standard' rate is 10%.

Transport

By air: SAS, the major Scandinavian carrier, has domestic services to Arvidsjaur, Gällivare, Gothenburg, Halmstad, Helsingborg, Jönköping, Kalmar, Kiruna, Karlstad, Luleå, Linköping, Malmö, Norrköping, Örebro, Sundsvall, Skellefteå, Umeå, Visby, Västerås and Växjö. Skyways operates to some of these, and also to some smaller airports. Braathens Malmö also operates some services.

COUNTING	
0	noll
1	ett
2	två
3	tre
4	fyra
5	fem
6	sex
7	sju
8	åtta
9	nio
10	tio
100	hundra
1000	tusen

By train: There is an excellent rail service across the country, mostly operated by SJ (Sveriges Järnväg – Swedish State Railways), but not exclusively so as there are four other train-operating companies, with much smaller networks. The famous Inlandsbanan, the inland railway, which operates northwards from Mora is not SJ. SJ operates the X2000 trains which run at up to 200kph (125mph) and link Stockholm with Gothenburg, Malmö, and a number of other large towns.
By bus: Swebus Express operates cross-country routes including services linking Stockholm with Malmö and Gothenburg and such exotic trips as Gothenburg to Gävle (and, for those looking to 'do' Scandinavia in one, Copenhagen to Oslo via Gothenburg). These services are supplemented by local carriers who operate to the smaller towns and villages. These more local services are good, but can be limited in number.
By road: Sweden has a good

CONVERSION CHART		
FROM	TO	MULTIPLY BY
Millimetres	Inches	0.0394
Metres	Yards	1.0936
Metres	Feet	3.281
Kilometres	Miles	0.6214
Square kilometres	Square miles	0.386
Hectares	Acres	2.471
Litres	Pints	1.760
Kilograms	Pounds	2.205
Tonnes	Tons	0.984
To convert Celsius to Fahrenheit: x 9 ÷ 5 + 32		

road system, though drivers should beware of the green roads marked on Swedish maps. There are two sorts – clearly indicated on the map, but easily overlooked. Not all green roads are motorways (i.e. they are dual carriageway). Some are 'ordinary' roads, though they are usually wide, allowing opportunities for overtaking. In many cases the road will have a broken white line near the verge: if a faster car comes up behind you, you must move into this space to allow overtaking. The new road over Öresund is a toll bridge: the booths are at the Swedish end and take Swedish or Danish cash, or credit cards. Sweden drives on the right, after transferring from left to right a few years ago. Headlights must be on at all times (hire cars have this facility built in; if you are in your own vehicle, remember to turn them off when you park). Seat belts are compulsory for all occupants. Children under seven years of age must be secured in a child seat or approved restraint. Motorcyclists must wear crash helmets. Speed cameras are not allowed in Sweden (though this is likely to change), but the police can, and do, have hand-held radar speedguns and hand out on-the-spot fines which are expensive and non-negotiable. The speed limits are: 50kph in towns and built-up areas, 70kph on minor roads, 90kph on major roads, 110kph on motorways and remote highways. The blood alcohol limit is 0.02%.

This is very low. It is also rigorously imposed and the penalties are non-trivial, with hefty fines and prison sentences. Driving in Sweden, outside of the big cities, is a pleasure as there is little traffic and the scenery is wonderful. The downside is that elk cross the roads. Every year animals are killed, and as the elk is a huge animal collisions can cost human lives and often do considerable damage to cars. Various ideas have been tried, the most visionary being the spraying of wolf urine on the verges of accident blackspots

to discourage the elk. When you see the 'Beware of Elk' signs please exercise caution. **By bicycle:** For local exploration, even in the cities, bicycles are great. They are very useful on Öland and Gotland.

Business Hours

Shops are usually open from 09:00–18:00 weekdays and 09:00–13:00 on Saturdays. However, in most towns with large numbers of visitors, and those geared to tourist trade, the closing time is often later. Businesses usually open 09:00–17:00 Mon–Fri (some

close at 15:00 in summer);
banks open 09:30–15:00
weekdays (16:00 on Thu).

Time Differences

Sweden operates on Central
European Time which is one
hour ahead of Greenwich
Mean Time (GMT). Daylight
saving sees the clocks move an
hour forward on the last Sunday in March and an hour back
on the last Sunday in October.

Communications

There are **post offices** in all
towns and large villages. They
normally keep shop hours.
There are public **telephones**
in most towns – particularly at
train and bus stations. These
usually only take phonecards –
available at post offices, kiosks
and some newsagents. The
code for international calls is
00, followed by the country
code. The country code for
Sweden is 46. Phone numbers
beginning 020 and 0200 are
free-phone. There are **inter-
net** facilities in most towns.

Electricity

Sweden has a 50Hz, 220V AC
electricity system utilizing the
standard continental two-pin
plug. UK visitors will need a
three-pin to two-pin adapter.
Visitors from North America
with 110V/115V appliances
will need a transformer.

Weights and Measures

Sweden uses the metric system of weights and measures,
(kilogram, metre, litre). On the
roads distances are measured
in kilometres and speed limits
are given in kph.

Health Precautions

Sweden is a healthy place
where it is safe to drink the
water and the chances of having stomach upsets or catching
curious illnesses are minimal.

Health Services

The Swedish health system is
complicated. For both major
and minor problems call at
the local hospital. As previ-
ously noted, EU visitors should
carry their E111 forms. All
visitors should understand
the terms and conditions of
their medical insurance.

Personal Safety

Sweden is as safe as any European country and so the
usual rules of safety should
be applied – do not leave
valuables on display in parked
cars, use safety deposit boxes
in hotels and be careful in
crowded city areas or when
travelling at night. As with all
developed countries Sweden
has a drug problem and this
brings petty crime in its wake.
The rules of safety you apply in
your own country should see
you safely through your visit.

Emergencies

For ambulance, fire service
and police, telephone 112.

Etiquette

Swedes are friendly and help-
ful and the normal rules of a
polite, civilized society apply.
The Swedes queue well and
do not appreciate queue-
jumpers. Knowing the
Swedish words for 'please'
and 'thank you' is appreciated
(see page 125).

Language

Swedish is a Scandinavian
language derived from the
original Viking language,
itself a Germanic tongue.
Danes, Norwegians and
Swedes can talk to each other
in their own languages and
be understood, differences
being similar to dialects in
other languages. By contrast,
Icelanders who talk a
language virtually identical to
the Viking tongue can neither
understand nor be under-
stood. Most Swedes speak
very good English. Swedish
has all the letters of the
English alphabet plus three
more – ä, ö and å.
The Sámi language is quite
separate from Swedish, being
derived from the Finno-Ugric
family. There are five different
Sámi languages (or dialects)
spoken in Sweden, the main
one being *Fell Sámi*.

GOOD READING

- **Alderton, Mary** *Blue Guide to Sweden.*
- **Berlin, Peter** *Xenophobe's Guide to the Swedes.*
- **Graham-Campbell, James** *The Viking World.*
- **Lagerlöf, Selma** *The Wonderful Adventures of Nils.*
- **Lindgren, Lyberg and Sandström, Wahlberg** *A History of Swedish Art.*
- **Scott, Franklin D** *Sweden: The Nation's History.*

INDEX

Note: Numbers in **bold**
indicate photographs

accommodation 48–49, 61,
  82–83, 89, 104–105, 115,
  121
Adventure Summerland 109
af Chapman 40, 41
Åhus 70, 71
Ales Stenar 14, 63, 70
Älvdalen 110, 115
Andrée, Salomon August
  99–100, **100**
Ängelsberg 51, 56
Aq-va-kul Water Park 66
Arctic Circle 5, 7, 117
Åre 107, 113, 115
Arjeplog 117, 118, 121
Årsunda 111–112
arts 25
Arvidsjaur 115, 117, 118,
  121
Åsensbruk 97
Askersund 59
Aspö Island 72
Åstol 91, 96
Astrid Lindgren's World 79
aurora borealis 5, 8, 119

Bastionen Konungen 71, **71**
Bengtsfors 97, 105
Bergs Slussar 81
birds 12, 69
Birka 15, 46
Björkborn Manor 59
Bjurholm 113
Blasieholmen 39
Blekinge 7, 63
Blomsholm 97
Bohuslän 91, 95–97
Boliden 114
Bönan 111
Borås 98
Borgholm 75, 83

Celsius, Anders 27, 55
Chinese Pavilion **45**, 46, 47
churches & cathedrals
  Helga Korskyrkan 71
  Helge And Kyrka 86
  Jacobs Kyrka 38, **38**

churches & cathedrals (cont)
  Lund Cathedral 63, 66–67,
    67
  St Maria Kyrkan 71
  Riddarholmskyrkan 36
  St Petri Kyrka 65
  Storkyrkan 36
  Trefaldighetskyrkan 71
cinema 27
climate 9–11, 39, 48, 52,
  61, 64, 82, 86, 89, 98,
  104, 109, 115, 118, 121
cuisine 28–29, 76

Dalarna 108–111
Dalén, Nils Gustav 27–28
Dalsland 91, 97
Djurgården 41–42
Djurpark 76
Dorotea 114
drinks 29
Drottningholm 45–46, **45**
Drottningskärs Kastell 72

Ebbas House 65–66
economy 20–22
Ekoparken 44
Ekornavallen 14, 91, 100
Ekshärad 60
Eriksberg Safari Park 71
Eskilstuna 51, 57, 61

Falkenberg 92, 103
Falköping 100
Falsterbo Peninsula 69
Falun 5, 8, **106**, 107, 108,
  108, 115
Fårö 85, 87, 88, **88**
fauna 11–12
flag 21, **21**
flora 11–12
food see cuisine
Funäsdalen 113

Gagnef 109
Gällivare 117, 119, 121
Gamla Stan **9**, **22**, **33**,
  33–36
Gamla Uppsala **24**, **50**, 51,
  52, **53**
Gästrikland 111–112
Gävle 107, 111, 115
Gesunda 109–110
Glasriket 77, 83

glass 63, 77, **77**, 83
Glimmingehus 70
Glösäbacken 107, 113
Göta Canal 5, 7, 19, **19**, 64,
  81, **81**, 91, 101, **101**, 105
Götaland 7, 91
Göteborg see Gothenburg
Götheborgs-Utkiken 94–95
Gothenburg 7, **19**, **20**, **90**,
  91, **92**, **95**, 104, 105
Gotland 8, **84**, 85–89
government 20–21
Gränna 63, 91, 99, 105
Gripsholm Slott 58
Grisslehamn 54
Grönklitt 110
Gunnebo Slott 102
Gyllenhjelmsgatan 51, 58
Gysinge 107, 111

Halland 92, 102–103
Hällefors 60
Halmstad 92, 103, **103**,
  104, 105
Hälsingland 112
Håverud 97
Hedemora 108
Hedmanska Gården 66
Helgeandsholmen 36–37
Helsingborg 63, 68, **68**, 82,
  83
Hemmistjörn 114
history 12–20, 31–33
Hornborgasjön 91, 101
Huskvarna 99

Ice Age 6, 12
Ice Globe Theatre 117
Ice Hotel 117, 121

Jacob Hansen's House 68
Jarl, Birger 16, **16**, 31, 32,
  36
Jokkmokk 117, 118–119,
  121
Jönköping 91, 98, 104, 105

Kaknäs Tower 44
Kalmar **62**, 63, **73**, 73–74,
  82, 83
Kalmar Slott **17**, 73–74
Kalmar Union 17–18, 73
Karlsborg 101
Karlshamn 71

Karlskoga 59, 61
Karlskrona 63, 71–72, **72**,
  82, 83
Karlstad 52, 60, 61
Kärnan Tower 68, **68**
Kastellholmen 41
Kebnekaise 7, 120
Kiruna 6, 8, 117, 121
Kivik 14, 70
Klädesholmen 96
Kolmården Djurpark 80
Kopparberg 51, 56–57
Koster islands 97
Kristianstad 71, **71**, 83
Kronan 74, 75
Kungliga Slottet **30**, 31,
  33–35, **34**
Kungsholmen 44
Kvarnholmen 74

Läckö Slott 101
Lagerlöf, Selma 26, 60, **60**
Landskrona 67
language 23
Lappland **116**, 117–120, 121
Lappstaden 117, 118
Lärbro 88, 89
Leksand 109, 115
Lidköping 91, 101
Lilla Torg 66, **66**
Lindgren, Astrid 26, 35, 63,
  79
Linköping 80, 82, 83
Lisebergs 91, 95
literature 25–26
Livrustkammaren 35
Longstocking, Pippi 35, 79
Ludvika 111, 115
Luleå 107, 114, **114**, 115
Lummelunda 85, 87
Lund 63, 66–67, 83
Lundagård Park 67
Lycksele 114, 115

Malmberget 117, 119
Malmö **4**, 6, 64–66, 82, 83
Malmöhus **4**, 64, 65, **65**,
  66
Malung 110–111
Mariefred 58
Mästarnas Park 60
Milles Gården **46**, 47
Mollösund 96–97
Mora 109, 115

museums 35, 92
  Ajtte Museum 119
  Arbetets Museum 80
  Arkitekturmuseet 40
  Biologiskamuseet 43
  Blekinge Museum 72
  Dansmuseet 37
  Ebelingmuseet 57
  F-11 Museet 59
  Filmmuseet 71
  Fredriksdal 68
  Gamla Linköping 80
  Gothenburg Konstmuseet
    91
  Gotlands Fornsal 85, 87
  Gripemuseet 59
  Gustav III's Antiquities
    Museum 35
  Historiska Museet 31, 41
  Konstmuseet 53, 92, 93
  Kultiven 67
  Läns Museum 74
  Maritime Museum 72,
    92
  Medelhavsmuseet 37
  Medeltidsmuseet 37
  Moderna Museet 40, **40**
  Museifartygen 43
  Museum of Sports 66
  Music Museum 38
  Näktergalen 79
  National Museum 39
  Natural History Museum
    92
  Nordiskamuseet 42, **42**
  Östasiatiska Museet 40
  Röhsskamuseet 92
  Rooseum 66
  Roslagen Museum 54
  Sjöfartsmuseum 74
  Skansen 31, 43
  Stadsmuseum 80
  Swedish National Portrait
    Gallery 58
  Swedish Royal Air Force
    Museum 80
  Tre Kronor Museum 35
  Universeum Science
    Discovery Centre 92
  Uppland Museum 53
  Vagnmuseet 65
  Vallby Friluftsmuseum 55
  Vapentekniskamuseet 57
  Vasamuseet 31, 42–43

museums (cont)
  Västerås Art Museum 55,
    55
  Vida Museum 76
music 26–27

Nääs Slott 100
national parks 8–9
  Abisko 9, 120
  Arctic national parks 117,
    120
  Blå Jungfrun 9, 78
  Färnebofjärden 9, 107,
    111
  Gotska Sandön 9, 87
  Muddus 119
  Padjelanta 9, 120
  Sarek 5, **8**, 9, 117, 120
  Stenshuvud 9, 70
  Stora Sjöfallets 120
  Store Mosse 9
  Tiveden 59
  Töfsingdalen 110
  Vadvetjåkka 9
nature reserves
  Getterön 103
  Mårdseleforsarna 113
  Neptuni Åkrar 75
  Västanå 99
Nobel, Alfred 28, 59
Norrköping 14, 63–64,
    79–80, **80**, 82, 83
Norrtälje 54, **54**
northern lights see aurora
    borealis
Nusnäs 110
Nyköping 51–52, 58–59, **59**,
    61

Öland 75–76
Opera House 37–38, **38**
Örebro 52, 61
Örebro Castle 51, 52, **56**
Örnsköldsvik 113
Örträsk 114
Östergötland 63, 91
Östersund 107, **112**,
    112–113, 115
Ottenby 76

Parken Zoo 57
people 22–28
planetarium 67
population 7, 33

Rådhuset 65, 68, **68**
Ramlösa Brunnspark 68
Raoul Wallenbergs Torg 39
Rättvik **18**, 109, 115
reindeer 12, **12**, **120**
religion 24
Reptile Centre 66
restaurants 49, 61, 83, 89,
    104–105, 115, 121
Riddarholmen 36
Riksbank 36
riksdag 19, 21, 23
Riksdagshuset 36
Rönneberg 60
Rosersbergs Slott 47
Royal Dramatic Theatre 38
Royal Palace, Stockholm see
    Kungliga Slottet

Sala 51, 55
Sälen 110
Sámi 23, 25, 117, 118, 121
Santaworld 110
science 27–28
Sergels Torg **32**, 38
shopping 61, 83, 89, 105,
    115, 121
Sigtuna 46–47
Sigurdsristningen 51, 57
Skåne 7, **7**, **17**, 63
Skåne Zoo 67
Skara 100
Skellefteå 107, 114, 115
Skeppsholmen 40–41
Skövde 101, 105
Slottsteater 45
Småland 7, 63
Smögen 91, 96, **96**, 97
Smygehuk 70
Sörmland 57–59
Steninge Slott 47
Stockholm 30–49
Storsjön Lake 107, 112
Stortorget 36, **36**
Strängnäs 51, 58, **58**
Strindberg, August 25–26
Strömstad 97, 105
Sundsvall 107, 112–113, 115
Svaneholm 69

Tåkern Lake 81
Tallås 112
Tännforsen 107, 113
Tanumshede 97, 105

Tärnaby 114
Tessinska Palatset 35
Tivoli amusement park 43
Tjöholm Slott 103
Tjörn 96
Torshälla 57
Torups Slott 68
tourist information 49, 61,
    83, 89, 105, 115, 121
tours 49, 61, 83, 89, 105,
    115, 121
Trädgårdsföreningens 94, **90**
transport 48, 61, 82, 89,
    104, 115, 121
Trelleborg 63, 69, **69**, 82
Treiksröset 118, **118**
Trollhättan 96
Trossö Island 72

Uddevalla 97
Umeå 107, 113, 115
Uppland 52–54
Uppsala 51, 53, 61

Vadstena 63, 81, 82, 83
Vänern Lake 7, 91
Vänersborg 96, 105
Varberg 102–103
Värmland 59–60
Vasa 42–43, **43**
Vasaloppet ski race 109, 110
Västerås 51, 55, 61
Västergötland 91, 98–102
Västervik 78, **78**, 83
Västmanland **6**, 55–57
Vättern Lake 7, 63, 81
Vaxholm 47
Vaxholm Castle **47**
Växjö 77, 82
Vikingabyn 85, 88
Vikings 15–17, 23, 88
Vimmerby 63, 79, 82, 83
Visby 5, 85, 86–87, 89
von Linné, Carl 27, 53, 61
Vuollerim 117, 118

Wik Slott 54
windmills 75, **75**
winter festival 118–119

Ystad 69–70, 71, 82, 83

zoos 67, 80
Zorn, Anders 26, **26**